COMING IN FIRST

Have a great year!

Jack

COMING
IN
FIRST

TWELVE KEYS TO
BEING A WINNER EVERY DAY

Jack H. Llewellyn, Ph.D.
with J. Donald McKee

Longstreet Press
Atlanta

Published by
LONGSTREET PRESS, INC.
2140 Newmarket Parkway
Suite 122
Marietta, GA 30067

Printed in the United States of America

1ˢᵗ printing 2000

Library of Congress Catalog Card Number: 00-105068

ISBN: 1-56352-630-1

Jacket and book design by Burtch Bennett Hunter

THIS BOOK IS DEDICATED TO MY WONDERFUL FAMILY —
JULIE, HUNTER, TRIPP, TATE, AND ABBY — FOR GIVING REAL
MEANING TO MY LIFE . . . AND TO SABLE FOR BEING
SO SPECIAL TO ALL OF US.

TABLE OF CONTENTS

COMING
IN
FIRST

INTRODUCTION

The Challenge:
Play to Not Lose — or Play to Win?

THE KEYS ARE WITHIN YOU

The keys to success in every aspect of your life are within you. These keys are called by many names, but they all boil down to one word: *Winning.* Winning over worry. Winning over obstacles. Winning on the job. Winning in life. The very word gives you a lift. When you win, you want to keep on winning.

By following the principles of *Coming In First*, developed in almost 30 years of on-hands experience and real-life laboratories with people as the subjects, you can find fulfillment, personally and professionally. The secret is in these two simple sentences:

Winners play to win. Survivors play to not lose.

If you don't play to win, don't play the game. That's my philosophy, but in my experience with athletes and business executives, working men and women, parents and kids, I have discovered a disturbing fact. Too many people are drifting along, hanging on, playing to not lose and to just survive. Winners are becoming harder to find because more people are playing not to lose instead of playing to win — on their jobs, in their families, in their personal lives. This is a dangerous mindset.

Why do so many people settle for survival when winning is so much better? The answer to this question is complex, but by analyzing the answer, you will begin to prepare yourself for a life of winning, not merely surviving. This chapter helps you to understand why you do what you do, and whether you are playing to not lose in life or playing to win.

THE SURVIVAL INSTINCT: BECOME INVISIBLE

The survival instinct is basic to our nature, but too many times it makes people try to become invisible and blend in with the surroundings like a chameleon or to assume a totally defensive posture like a tortoise hiding in its shell, rather than taking on the challenge and risking failure or defeat. It can keep you from being a winner.

Here's how it works: A major corporation decided to cut 20,000 people from its payroll worldwide, a life-changing challenge for those people losing their jobs and one that affected their attitude toward surviving in a downsizing corporate world. Yet many of them would go on to find better jobs, more rewarding careers in their own businesses or enjoy the fruits of retirement. The cutbacks also presented major concerns for the remaining employees, a point not grasped by senior management at the time.

My question to an officer of the corporation was: "What will happen to the 50,000 people who are left in the company?" The answer: "They will still have jobs."

"That's a terrible answer," I said. "If you cut 20,000, then you've got at least another 20,000 of their friends who are going to be just surviving for the next six months to a year, and another 10,000 or so are going to be wondering if they will be let go next."

About two months after that meeting, I was on a flight to Atlanta where my seatmate turned out to be regional vice president for marketing of the downsizing company.

"What do you do?" I asked.

"Nothing," she said.

"Nothing? What do you mean 'nothing'?"

"You might have read that we've cut 20,000 people," she said. "So I'm just trying to stay invisible because I don't want to be next."

My first thought was, *How many people are there like that in the company's management, in positions with influence over the workforce? How many people throughout the company are just trying to stay out of the way so they won't be noticed, so they won't be next?*

For the sake of the company's future, if I'd been the consultant, I would have counseled: "You need to tell these people they're winners. They're not survivors. They're still on the job because they are the people who will take your company to the next level. They need to rally around each other and raise the productivity of everyone."

As it happened, the company made a smart move and retained a firm to create a program for the people who kept their jobs. The firm in charge of the "those-who-were-left" program ordered T-shirts, caps, buttons, pencils and notepads for distribution to the employees. You would have expected all of those items to carry an upbeat, aggressive message for the people facing the huge challenge of setting things right in the company after thousands of their fellow workers had been dismissed.

But guess what was the theme emblazoned on every T-shirt and cap, the buttons, pencils and notepads? "The Survivors."

Unbelievable. These people were being programmed to just hang on. Like too many other people, they were getting the message that survival is okay, even though it was an unintended consequence.

What is surviving? It's drifting along, taking the easy way, the course of least resistance, not rocking the boat, not challenging the status quo, not taking risks.

SURVIVAL CONDITIONING: IN THE BOTTOM OF THE BOX

A lot of people learn to feel good about just surviving. It begins to taste good, and it begins to be very comfortable.

It's like the puppies in a box. When I was a youngster growing up in the country, our dog had a litter, and we put the puppies in a box by the kitchen stove, the warmest spot in the house. We fed the puppies there, watered them there, took care of them there in the box. Every once in a while, one of the puppies would stick his head up over the side of the box as if he was going to get out and run through the house. One of us boys would give that pup a little rap and push him back down in the box. The other puppies would take long looks at their sibling as if they were thinking, "You know, I'm not getting out of this box today. I'm not taking any chances. I'm going to stay right here in the bottom of the box."

A week later when we cut down the sides of the box, where did those puppies go? Nowhere. They stayed in the bottom of the box where it was secure. They got their food and water there. They were with each other there. So they learned to live in the bottom of the box.

It's training. It's conditioning. It's something we put animals through. But in reality, many people live their lives that way. They learn to be survivors, content to live in the bottom of the box.

The problem with just surviving is that it lets you get by, earn enough money to pay the bills, to take a vacation, to save for retirement and then to feel that you've done all right. But you are just surviving.

If, on the other hand, you want to win, and you play to win every day, both professionally and personally, then you move to a higher level. You do the things that are necessary to get you to the next level.

The problem is that people are conditioned or programmed for surviving, not winning. They are programmed by adults and parents, who send the wrong messages to children. They are programmed by our educational system, which tolerates and even promotes survival. They are programmed by many corporate cultures to just survive, not to win.

The truth is that we are all given too much negative conditioning. In many cases, parents unwittingly start programming their children to just survive from the day they're born. It's human nature, trying to keep the children from making mistakes, trying to put them in error-free, protected environments, never allowing or enabling the children to learn how to recover from adversity or failure.

Children learn to work at *not failing*. They go to school, and the same thing happens. Then one day they're in the workforce and, of course, they're still playing to not lose every day. They take the easy way out. They stay in the bottom of the box.

The attitude of playing or working or living to *not lose* causes your performance to decline, many times so subtly that you don't really notice until it undermines your dignity and self-respect. If you are just surviving — trying to not lose, always taking a defensive posture — you won't ever get to the point where you truly understand why you do what you do. You will never realize the fulfillment that comes from performing at the next level.

WINNING: A DIFFERENT WORLD

Winning is not easy. It is challenging, demanding and costly. It's risky. It's sometimes lonely. It's even frightening at times. Deciding to be a winner is a tough decision to make. You can't delegate it to somebody else. It's not a corporate decision. It's not a departmental decision. It's not even a decision that a couple can sit down and make.

Winning is a personal decision that you have to make for yourself. And once you buy into winning as opposed to just surviving, then your world is going to change dramatically.

YOU'RE GOING TO BE HAPPIER.

Winners tend to be happier people. They are not necessarily those with the most money, but they are appreciative for what they have in life. They feel blessed for everything that has come their way. They are less stressed, and if they are stressed, they learn to deal with it as a constructive force. They understand the meaning of "balance," which is a critical factor for winning. Winners usually have loving families, and they have strong, sincere support systems in place.

You see that winning versus surviving is not about money. It's not about material gain. It's not about having the right house in the right neighborhood, or the right car or the right country club membership. You cannot look at financial statements and determine who are the winners and who are the losers. That is a very shallow way to keep a scorecard of our lives.

WINNING, IF IT IS UNDERSTOOD, IS A LIFETIME TASK.

The game is never over. If you win, if you achieve, if you succeed, then you earn the right to take a deep breath and move to the next level. It is a lifelong process, just as learning is. You win from having tried to learn something every day.

A few years ago I was invited to speak at a church service on Sunday morning, and I talked about "Winning versus Surviving" to a group of the older folks. The youngest was about 75 and the oldest probably 95. I told them, "It's very important to play to win every day, regardless of how old you are. If you're a hundred you can win. If you're breathing, you can win by helping somebody else or helping yourself."

After the service, the minister thanked me and said, "That was a very unusual speech for these people."

"What do you mean?" I asked.

"You talked to them about winning," he said. "The only things anybody else ever talks to them about are death and salvation."

Regardless of what the conventional approach might be, I felt that those people, like everyone else, needed to think about winning, whatever their ages. Many of them, if not all of them, benefited from thinking about winning, from thinking that they had something to offer others from their years of living.

WINNING IS ALL ABOUT HAVING FULFILLMENT IN YOUR LIFE.
Winning is about fulfilling your basic needs, about doing the right things for the right reasons. For example, if you play a game as an athlete and you happen to win by a close score, you won on the scoreboard. But did you actually play as well as you could possibly play? Or did you walk away and leave energy on the field? If you lost the game by a close score, does that mean you really lost? Did you do everything you possibly could and then walk away, having used all your assets? If so, you might have won personally. You might have achieved something you never achieved before. *That is winning.*

A five-year-old soccer player can run every minute of every game and afterward feel that he or she had a part in the game simply because he or she got as tired as everyone else on the team — but avoided trying to kick the ball at all costs. Maybe the reason was that his or her self-concept wasn't developed. The self-confidence wasn't there until that kid was part of what was going on. Yet the five-year-old won because of participation and energy invested. It may be that in the seventh or eighth game, the same youngster jumps out and tries to kick the ball.

You win at different levels, and once you get confidence and self-concept, then you move up to the next level. You always try to achieve more than you achieved the last time. You need to understand and define winning for yourself, but your definition must cause you to stretch your capabilities on a daily basis.

Misconceptions about winning proliferate in the workplace; for example, to win you have to have more money, work longer hours and bend or break the rules. These ideas are generally accepted. But they are not what it takes to become a real winner. As I discuss in *Key 10*, we in corporate America need to create an environment in which people want to win but also want to play by the rules.

DEFINING WHAT WINNING REALLY MEANS

If you don't understand why you do what you do, you may not truly understand winning or surviving. In order to win, you must understand why you do what you do, and you must understand the meaning of reward and when a reward is appropriate.

Have you ever watched a T-ball game or a Little League game or "beehive soccer," soccer for five-year-olds? These environments can help you to understand many concepts. Winning, surviving, appreciation of your team, interaction and influencing people all can be learned by watching kids on the field of play.

For several years I traveled around the country working with parents of youth soccer groups. In my view soccer, potentially, is the best sport available for children, because of the coordination and the teamwork demanded, plus the constant motion that exercises the entire body. But these benefits depend on the parents, the kids and their coaches taking the correct attitude toward the game.

A California group invited me to a state championship match of five-year-old soccer players. The tournament was to be a wonderful experience, especially when the trophies were given out. They were so huge that the kids couldn't carry them, but the parents could, and that seemed to be the critical thing.

The game was unforgettable. It was almost over, and the score was 2-1. The contest resembled a beehive. Twenty kids piled up in the center of the field. Late in the game, the pile of kids moved in front of one of the goals. If that team scored, the game would be tied 2-2, and it would go to overtime. I had to see how the goalkeeper was handling the stress of 20 combatants not 10 feet away and hordes of parents screaming on both sides of the field.

At his end of the field, the five-year-old goalkeeper was down on one knee. He was tying his shoe, which for the typical kid that age is a very difficult task. So the kid was really working at it. He didn't even know 20 kids were 10 feet away from him. He finished tying his shoe, looked at it, and a bell went off in his head. He had to show somebody. He ran to the sidelines to show his mom and left the goal unattended. When he held up his shoe, his mom started screaming at him: "We're going to lose! You're giving up the tying goal! You'll embarrass your father and me! We'll have to move out of southern California!" The kid looked at his shoe, hung his head and ran back into position at the goal.

Just as he crouched in front of the goal, the whistle sounded and the game was over. His teammates picked him up and carried him off the field. He was waving at the crowd with a big smile. "I learned to tie my shoe today," he was thinking. "It's a big day in my life." And it was.

That night at the board meeting of the soccer organization, I stood up and asked, "Why do you have goalkeepers in five-year-old soccer? They never get to play, never get to kick. You put the most awkward kids in the position, and consequently, they never even learn to run."

Every member of the board held up the rulebook. "It's the way it's supposed to be played. We have to have a goalkeeper."

"What would happen if you took them out?"

"The score would be 10 to 15," somebody said.

"If it is 10 to 15," I asked, "how many kids win as opposed to the score being 2 to 1? In a five-year-old's mind, winning is probably perceived as being able to kick the ball in the goal."

The board members sat and thought about it for a while. Then they agreed to try it in the spring. They did, and every Saturday game was like a picnic. It became a big family get-together where all the kids played. They learned the same skills they'd learned before. They kicked the ball in the goal, and the parents threw the ball back. It was a rewarding experience for everyone.

Changing the rules to create a different perspective meant all the kids were winners. Today in at least two national soccer leagues, there is no goalkeeper in five- and six-year-old play. Every kid is a winner. But before that was possible, we had to change the rules, we had to redefine what winning meant.

WHAT'S MISSING: OPEN COMMUNICATION

There is a tremendous lack of open and honest communication among people, especially in corporate America. We have stopped talking face-to-face. We no longer verbalize to each other. We can boast about how e-mail enables us to reach more people or we can extol the virtues of the fax machine. But these innovations mean we don't talk as much as we once did in order to communicate effectively. Consequently, our support systems are not functioning as they once were.

In some companies that I have visited, I have seen people send e-mail across the room or across the hall. In some cases, employees have told me they had a conflict with their supervisor. When I asked where the supervisor was located, it turned out he or she was a partition away, almost within arm's reach, maybe three feet at most. But these people never talked to each other. They e-mailed back and forth.

There is no way you can understand winning or develop a support system to help you win if you never talk with other people who are a part of that support system.

I attended one corporate meeting of vice presidents, a relatively quiet meeting, but I noticed a lot of people biting their lips. After it was over, all of the participants rushed back to their desks, jumped on their computer keyboards and e-mailed their reactions to everybody else who was in the meeting. There was no exchange of emotions, no give-and-take.

There was an exchange of messages. Nothing was resolved.

Winning requires wholesome communication, which is part of any healthy environment. It means looking forward to conflict and the management of conflict, to dealing with crises, not only individually but within a group. Winners communicate. Survivors send messages.

CHECKLIST FOR WINNERS

1. You must have a strong foundation. In other words, you need to understand why you do what you do. You must know your own personality and traits — which things will help you win, which ones keep you at a survivor level. You need to understand your core values, and that this foundation does not change.

2. You must have a basic personal philosophy of life that answers these questions: How am I going to live my life? How am I going to support other people in winning? What is the philosophy within my family? How am I going to raise my children? What are the things I would like for them to understand and to believe? It is important, in order to win, to have strong convictions, to believe in something.

3. You must have a strong sense of ethics, an ability to play by the rules. You need to accept the fact that defeat is part of life and learn to recover from it and profit from it. You need to be humble as a winner and not to degrade those who play to win but don't win.

4. You need to have balance in your life. You must understand that you cannot give up balance in your life to win on one side and lose on the other. When someone tells me he's very proud he has worked 18 hours a day for his whole career, I consider that person may have a mental dysfunction. In my professional opinion, there is no reason to work 18 hours a day for your whole life. There is no reason that I can think of for you to put your life in your job, because jobs come and go. Once you begin to understand why you do what you do, you realize that you do your job to support the personal side of your life. You cannot lose sight of that. And when I talk about balance, it is not in terms of hours spent but in terms of quality.

5. You must have talent to win. There is no question that talent is a prerequisite to winning. Granted, a lot of speakers rake in big money asserting that "If you can visualize it, you can do it." However, that is incorrect. You must have talent to execute.

There are many things I can visualize that I cannot execute, such as hitting a 300-yard drive down the center of the fairway. I can visualize it but even on my best day of golf, I could not execute a 300-yard drive, no matter which direction it went. I also visualize throwing a 95-mile-per-hour fastball when I'm in the Braves spring training camp. But if I throw the ball and it's timed by the speed gun, about 48 mph is all I can do. So don't tell me that "whatever you can visualize, you can execute." Before you start visualizing winning, you must have assessed the talents and skills you bring to the endeavor.

6. At the same time, you must be a risk taker to win. You need to put yourself on the line, to stretch your system. Survivors

never stretch their system, never take risks or get into conflict or crisis. Many of them do all right. But when their company decides to move to a higher level, they get left behind. Golfers who play at a low level of competition can go out and shoot 67 or 68 because there's no pressure, nothing significant on the line. Take those same players and put them in a professional golf tournament where a three-foot putt could be worth $100,000, and they shoot 72 or 73 in the first round and fail to make the cut. The world is filled with great "practice players," who are best when nothing is at stake. Very few people can win in the tough situations fraught with conflict and crisis. To be a winner, you need to thrive on stress, to look forward to things that will stretch your system and make you better.

7. Finally, a small but important point: You must listen as much or more than you talk. Listening is the forgotten form of communication. Understanding what the other person is trying to say is absolutely crucial to winning.

CHANGE YOUR MINDSET: START WINNING

I've worked with elite performers for many years. I've seen them change the way they get to the top and metamorphose from survivors into winners. In 1991 John Smoltz, a promising young pitcher with the Atlanta Braves, had a dismal record of only two wins against 11 losses. This pitcher had begun to play not to lose. Eventually, he would have become a survivor, but at this point he wasn't even that good. He was losing and, in frustration, had begun pitching defensively instead of pitching to win.

John and I started to work together. We spent a lot of time talking about recovering from adversity and why he did what he did, how to win, how to be successful, working on increasing the probability that he could win, changing his mindset from pitching to not lose — specifically trying to avoid throwing balls instead of concentrating on throwing strikes. In the second half of the season, John won 12 games and lost only two — the biggest turnaround by a pitcher in professional baseball in more than half a century. John went on to pitch brilliantly in the National League playoffs and in the seventh game of the World Series in 1991, and the Braves went from the worst team in 1990 to the best team in baseball in 1991 — from worst to first. The Braves kept winning, and won the division title year after year. John Smoltz has been an integral part of the team's winning record. He has had a tremendous influence on young pitchers in teaching them how to pitch to win, rather than pitching to not lose and how to recover from adversity.

Now John takes something extra with him to the mound on those days when he's not at the top of his game. Out of three pitches, maybe he will only have two pitches working. And he will still win. He wins because he wants to win. Other teams know this, although you can never tell from his expression whether he's winning or losing. But he is always doing what he has to do in order to succeed as a pitcher, to be a winner. He not only wants to win, but projects winning to other people, and it causes them to play better.

It's a major attitudinal upheaval for someone to quit playing the survival game, for him or her to come to the conclusion, "If I'm in the game, I might as well win." They will win as a result.

Why? The answer is not in changing anything mechanically — not the sequence of pitches or arm strength or the teams pitched against. None of that changes. What changes is the way this pitcher looked both at the game and at why he did what he did, and how he could use all his assets. In other words, his mindset changed from a survival mode, and he began to pitch to win. And not only did he win, but he began to enjoy the game and to realize true fulfillment from what he did on the mound.

The same thing has happened with many hitters who bought into the principles of my program and had the best years of their pro careers. Again, we never touched their mechanics. We didn't change their bats or how they hit, when they hit or whom they hit against. What we changed was the way they looked at themselves, the way they looked at the game and the way they looked at their assets. As a result, they stopped trying to perform against their liabilities, or trying to survive — playing to not lose — and they started performing with their assets, using their talents and playing to win.

That's the concept of *Coming In First*. You don't spend your time avoiding your liabilities. You spend your time flaunting your assets. Then you increase the probability that you will win. Using the concepts of this book will bring you to a better understanding of the steps you need to take to get where you want to go; to know when you arrive and to realize the fulfillment of becoming all that you had hoped; fulfilling needs that you never knew were there; and helping other people fulfill needs in their lives.

History supports the assumption that more people play

to not lose than play to win on a regular basis. Surviving is easier. Winning causes higher expectations. Accountability also increases. Many people are very uncomfortable with these aspects of winning and have translated their feeling into a basic fear of success. You can get stuck between the fear of success and the fear of failure, never moving one way or the other, personally or professionally.

GET RID OF THE SECURITY BLANKET!

Some people take their security blanket and wrap themselves in it. The only exposure they have to winning is when it's accidental and happens to come their way. You cannot be a winner unless you get rid of your security blanket. If you are thinking, "That is ridiculous, I gave up my security blanket along with my childhood," don't forget that security blankets come in many forms and in places you might not suspect.

What about the office or on the job?

On one occasion when I met with a board of directors of a corporation, I discovered the room was filled with security blankets. As is the usual arrangement, the chairman of the board occupied an imposing chair at the head of the conference table. Before any of the board members spoke, they waited until Mr. Chairman spoke. Then everyone agreed with whatever Mr. Chairman said. Afterward we went to lunch without the chairman, and even then every statement by a board member was to the effect, "Well, the chairman, he always says so-and-so." Everyone else would nod their heads in agreement.

It was an eerie environment. No one had an identity. Everybody was surviving, clinging to the security blanket, which in this case was the job. Here was a bunch of yes-men with no fulfillment, and all they had to anticipate was retiring after having accomplished nothing more than not being fired by the chairman.

How many people in the same situation find the courage to speak up, to take a stand, to toss the job security blanket out the window? If you faced this situation, what would you do? Would you go for security, for survival, or take a risk and go for winning?

YOU NEED TALENT AND MUCH MORE

Everyone has talents, which are basic to winning. But what distinguishes the winners from the survivors most of the time is not talent. It is the will to win, the mindset. This includes the ability to quickly recover from adversity and — one of the single biggest factors in winning — the development of positive emotion as a supplement to talent. Emotion is a tremendous supplement to talent. The same is true of hard work. It may not of itself make anyone a winner, but hard work combined with talents is the formula for winning.

Believing that you can win is half the battle!

Too few people are told they can win. Consequently, they never understand what it takes to win.

In my sport psychology program, success does not result from changing the athlete's mechanics, the physical process or methodology. Success comes from somewhere else. It begins when I sit down with an athlete in the first meeting and tell him or her: "I expect you to be able to make your assets better, to flaunt those assets and to remove your liabilities. I am not in the habit of setting myself or my program up to fail, and you will get better before this is over." The athlete, consequently, starts the program with a crucial element of success in place: the expectation of succeeding, of winning and not just surviving.

Winning is a lot more fun than just surviving. If you want to be a winner every day, keep reading.

KEY 1

Knowing Your Assets and Liabilities — and Winning

WINNING WITH YOUR ASSETS — AND YOUR LIABILITIES

What do you think of when you see the terms "assets" and "liabilities"? Most people immediately think of accounting and financial statements showing total net worth as measured by money, stocks and bonds, property and other material things. In this chapter, however, assets and liabilities are defined in less tangible terms. These assets and liabilities are possessed by every person, regardless of material possessions. All of us have *assets* — things on the positive side of the ledger, things we do well. All of us have *liabilities* — things on the negative side of the ledger, things that we would like to do better or things that we would like to remove from our personal balance sheet in order to be better.

How often do you observe people avoiding their liabilities,

hoping that something good will happen? Yet in my experience few people ever take the time to examine their assets or their liabilities in depth or in an organized way.

Of course, you feel more comfortable with your assets. You like to show them off or flaunt them, and you should. But you also need to recognize your liabilities and to share them with other people in order to become better, to make you stand out from the crowd and make your talents greater assets to yourself, your family, your company or the other important areas of life. It is the people in your personal life and your professional life, the people on your team, who can help you to remove liabilities or offset them.

For example, if you have five assets and five liabilities, and you sit down with a group of people with whom you work in close daily contact, you probably will find that each of those persons has at least one asset to offset one of your liabilities. If you are poorly organized, for example, chances are that a member of your group is super organized. That means you can walk away from the group with *ten assets* instead of five assets and five liabilities. If you get into difficulty because of one of your liabilities, you can call on someone who can offset that liability for you. A major benefit of recognizing both your positive and negative traits — your assets and liabilities — is that it makes you a better person personally and professionally. It also draws you closer to others. Rather than making you dependent, it places you in an interdependent kind of relationship in which you feel confident. Part of that confidence comes from knowing that you have a good support system. There is always someone who will either supplement your assets or help offset your liabilities.

It is a puzzle to me when people believe they can develop a plan to win — or succeed at their highest level — if they do not understand their assets and liabilities. We spend a lot of time developing goals, personally and professionally. We spend a lot of time talking about winning in some form. We spend a lot of time talking about our beliefs and philosophy and the need to change and to do numerous other things. But we spend very little time evaluating our assets and liabilities. Yet these are what make us fit into the different environments that constitute the world in which we invest our time and energy.

Of course, not many people enjoy putting their liabilities on the table for close scrutiny by colleagues or family members or friends. It takes courage to look at your liabilities, even when you're alone, but it is much more challenging to expose your areas of weakness to others. However, it is only by recognizing and working with your liabilities that you can remove them, offset them or neutralize them.

IT IS CRITICAL TO SHARE
YOUR ASSETS — AND LIABILITIES

Our corporate culture once was filled with top-heavy companies overloaded with management positions and large workforces. There were plenty of people in the environment to blame for failures. Many people never had to recognize or reveal their liabilities, but kept them safely tucked away from view. Since then, the corporate landscape has undergone a traumatic upheaval — "rightsizing," "downsizing," "reengineering" or whatever the current term may be. It means cutting back jobs, dismissing people. It demands more productivity from fewer people. Consequently, it means that everyone needs to share his or her assets and liabilities and that in the corporate environment, teams need to become much stronger.

Winners don't have the luxury of the blame game. The key is to become more productive, to be willing to share with those who have an impact on your life. Begin with the question: "Who has an impact on my life?" Sit down and take the time to look at your team: your personal team, those closest to you and your professional team, those in your work environment.

ANYONE WHO HAS ANY INFLUENCE OR IMPACT ON YOUR LIFE WHATSOEVER ALSO NEEDS TO BE FAMILIAR WITH YOUR ASSETS AND YOUR LIABILITIES.

That person may already be aware of your assets, but you must make certain that you share some of your liabilities and then develop team actions with that person and appropriate others to help you offset your liabilities. Either remove or overcome the liabilities or else learn to live with them, to control them to the best advantage. This applies to your personal environment especially as well as your work environment.

SHARING YOUR LIABILITIES LEADS TO MORE PRODUCTIVITY, MORE EFFICIENT AND EFFECTIVE TEAMWORK.

This concept of teamwork can be demonstrated by parents in dealing with their children. Typically, one parent is perceived by the children as being easy, and the other parent as the stronger disciplinarian. It does not have to be a problem, but rather it can help the couple to function as a team. It is important that the parents understand their traits in this respect and then present a unified front to the children. Consistency must be maintained. When there is a disciplinary action taken, the parent who is soft on discipline cannot, in talking with the child, undermine the action by indicating it was wrong or excessive. The discipline then loses all credibility, and the parent who is the stronger disciplinarian loses his or her credibility. The key is for the parents to work together, benefiting from each other's assets and offsetting each other's liabilities.

The same holds true in the corporate environment. A person with the liability of being a weak decision-maker must offset or eliminate that liability. If you are not a strong decision-maker, and people keep coming to you but do not get satisfactory decisions, they will make their own decisions. The key is to surround yourself with people who are strong decision-makers. Then make certain that when decisions are made and conveyed to the workforce, they are team decisions and you are consistent with them.

It is important that everyone recognizes his or her assets and liabilities — and the assets and liabilities of others on the team. It is not always necessary to change a person's assets and liabilities. Your assets are what you have, what "brought you to the party," and your liabilities are a part of you as well. Although there are some liabilities you can change or remove, others cannot be fixed, and you must not lose sleep over them. Instead, find individuals who can offset those liabilities for you.

This makes for a stronger team, whether it's your personal team or your professional team. The result will be improved performance and a more comfortable environment for you and your team. Sharing assets and liabilities will make the people around you feel more important. They feel they can offer something to the process, that they have something to give. They feel they can take more risks because someone can offset *their* liabilities and help them through the process. Productivity will increase with more efficient and effective teamwork. It does not matter if you are a one-person company or a single parent or an individual athlete. There is a team somewhere to which you can relate.

THERE IS A SUPPORT SYSTEM AVAILABLE

You may be a professional golfer. The general perception is that you are all by yourself in this sport. That is only partly true. Even though you alone take the swings to drive or putt the ball, there are many important steps that involve your team. These include the preparation for playing, both physically and mentally. A golfer might have a nutritionist, a weight trainer, a conditioning coach, a mechanics coach, a putting coach, a sports psychologist, a financial adviser, a promotion and marketing agent. There could be a team of eight to 10 people surrounding this golfer, not including his family and friends. All those people make up his team. The team could be as few as three or a dozen or more, but every person on it brings some asset or assets to make the team stronger and, therefore, improve the golfer's performance.

How many of your assets do you take for granted? Think for a moment about the hearing impaired. They don't have any extra physical features that enable them to see any better than normally sighted persons. Yet they do. They use to the fullest the optical assets they have. How many people with normal hearing read lips? Not very many, usually only those who have learned this skill in order to communicate with the hearing impaired. The rest of us don't have to use our assets in this way. So we don't. Sight-impaired people don't have any special physical abilities to make them hear better than those with vision, yet they do. They hear better because they use the auditory assets they have to help them communicate. You can do a lot more with your assets if you truly want to become better at what you do, to be a winner, not a survivor.

In a celebrity golf tournament, I was teamed with a foursome. As we played, we talked about sport psychology and golf, how various factors influence a golfer's shots. Ahead of us, a foursome of amateurs and a celebrity teed up. The hole was a par-3. It was about 150 yards long with a lake between the tee and the green. We stopped and watched.

Each of the amateurs prepared for his drive in the same way. Each put away his new ball and took out an old one from his bag, then stepped up to the tee and proceeded to knock the ball into the water. The balls landed so close together that you could have thrown a blanket over the spot.

Then the celebrity got ready. The first thing he did was to take a new ball out of his bag. He teed it up and swung his club. The ball landed within two feet of the cup. That is quite a feat for any golfer, but the most remarkable part of this perform-ance involved a liability of the celebrity player. He was blind.

The difference between the mindset of the amateurs and the celebrity was striking. The amateurs could see the water and, consequently, took out their old, expendable balls for the shot over the water, clearly signaling their expectations of the ball landing in the water from the outset. On the other hand, the blind player did not see the water and never tried to avoid it. He knew his assets and he used them to the fullest. He overcame his liabilities by using his assets.

On the 18th green all of the amateur players missed a putt. Then the blind celebrity stepped up and made his putt to win the tournament for them. They won because this gifted player was not influenced by peripheral things, the water, the sand traps, the people watching and all the other distractions that would bother most of us sighted golfers. This player became a great golfer, a winner for many years at one of the most difficult and demanding sports. He knew his assets and how to use them to become a winner, not a survivor.

COMMIT TO USING AND IMPROVING ALL YOUR ASSETS

For a baseball player having problems in hitting, my approach is to get the player to focus on his assets, not his liabilities: "Instead of going to bat and trying to not strike out or trying to avoid a pitch that you have problems with, which is a liability, why not look to hit the ball wherever it is pitched? If you have a good swing, that's an asset. So use it." For a pitcher struggling with the mindset of not throwing balls or bad pitches, my approach would be: "If your asset is a fast ball and your liability is a curve, why not use your assets in tough situations? Don't try to hide your liabilities. Acknowledge them."

In some cases I have seen pitchers who could mask their liabilities. One professional pitcher had a 79-mile-per-hour fastball. It was a liability, not an asset, because the average fastball for major league pitchers is almost 90 mph. But this pitcher had a great curve ball and a great change-up. He learned to throw the change-up, followed by his 79 mph fastball and then a breaking pitch that made the fast-ball look like it was 90 mph. He was able to catch his liabil-ity between assets and to make it an asset by the way he used it. He turned a negative stressor into a positive force for winning instead of surviving or losing.

Liabilities present a different kind of challenge than do assets. People either neglect their liabilities or spend so much time on them that they lose their assets in the process. It's like a student bringing home two A's and one D, then spending all his time in studying to change the D. As a result, on the next report card the student has two C's and one B. It is critical that while you are working on your liabilities that you develop actions to protect your assets.

WRITE DOWN YOUR ASSETS AND LIABILITIES

Be sure to write down your assets and liabilities using the worksheet at the end of this chapter. This exercise is absolutely essential. It is necessary in order for you to recognize your assets and liabilities in order for you to deal with them appro-priately, to take action to manage your liabilities, to protect your assets and to share this information with others. Only then will you be on the road to consistent winning.

Almost every list of assets and liabilities written by par-ticipants in the "Winning versus Surviving" program contains items that can be placed on both the asset and liability side.

The most common of these is emotion, which can be an asset but may often be a liability unless it is controlled. Aggressiveness, which should be an asset, can also be a liability. Confidence can be both an asset and a liability, depending on whether it is excessive and how it is perceived. Therefore, it is extremely important that you list your assets and liabilities and *place them in the category into which you would say they currently fall.* Then, assuming you have placed aggressiveness, for example, in the liability column, develop the actions needed to move it over to the asset list.

How assets can turn into liabilities was demonstrated by Atlanta Braves pitcher Tom Glavine during the 1994 strike by the players union. Glavine happened to be the representative of the union. Always well groomed and well dressed, he is very articulate and forthright — assets that made him a good subject for interviews but also an easy target for the anger of the fans. The very fact that he did his job as spokesman so confidantly was turned against him. He was perceived by hostile fans as representing greed and arrogance. His enviable talents, his assets, became liabilities.

Emotion becomes a liability instead of an asset when you are not performing well, and you don't know how to recover when you go over the edge emotionally. Thinking through a problem is an asset, but it becomes a liability if you think too much about what you are doing and this inhibits your performance. In sports, focusing on mechanics only is a liability.

Aggressiveness can be a tremendous asset. But if it is used in a negative way it is a tremendous liability. For example, a student may cause problems in the classroom setting because he is too aggressive and abrasive with others. But when the same student goes to the athletic field for practice and training at sport, if he is not aggressive he will be disciplined by his coach.

So much depends on the definition. You understand what assets are, and you understand what liabilities are. It is imperative that when you list your assets and liabilities that you also define them as you go. Then you are in position to take actions.

When I work with any individual, regardless of the environment, the first step is to have that person list his assets and liabilities. If I have any concern about his objectivity, then I ask those around him what they consider to be his assets and liabilities. From this list, I try to determine what the real assets and liabilities are.

Try this exercise as an experiment. If your communication has not been as good as it should be with other people — whether your spouse, children, a friend or people in your corporate environment — write down your assets and your liabilities. Then share them with another, spouse or friend, and make a constructive session out of your sharing. This will enable both of you to understand each other better.

When people list their assets and liabilities, their assets are usually dominated by physical qualities. This is especially true of athletes, who list such attributes as size, strength, speed, abilities, quickness, endurance and stamina. Mental assets often listed include such qualities as *dedicated, honest, achieving,* along with traits like "can stay focused for a long period" or "stay calmest when things aren't going well."

By contrast, liability lists usually include emotional factors or attitudes, as shown by this list from a participant in the "Winning versus Surviving" program: 1) tend to look at the negative things; 2) dwell on failures; 3) tend to picture negative experiences as opposed to mentally picturing positive experiences; 4) fear of the situation; 5) too much respect for the opposition; and 6) doubt my abilities.

When your liabilities are mostly mental, you should spend your time increasing your confidence level and your positive experiences. Then your asset list grows significantly. For instance, if you want to move "lack of confidence" from the liability side to "confidence" on the asset side, what actions should you take? One is to put yourself in a position to succeed more often. You must learn how to evaluate success more accurately. This doesn't mean you must change your job or your personal environment. When you learn to define "winning" more accurately, you learn to focus more on the process during performance. Analyze the process; dissect the parts. Success may lie in executing the "parts" correctly. You have now won for that particular day, even though someone else may prevail on the scoreboard.

One of my PGA golfers was in a position to win a tournament recently. As the day unfolded, a previous two-time winner of the tournament made a tremendous run of birdies and set a tournament-record low score. My golfer played exceptionally well on the final day. On the last hole he was tied with four other golfers for second place, with a very difficult 20-foot putt for birdie remaining — in front of a huge crowd and a national television audience. Making the putt would give him second place alone, and an additional $170,000. He stepped up and sank the putt. In that particular "part" of the process, he certainly won.

If your task has no priority order for completion, start with parts that will give you some gratification, which will lead to confidence as the parts become more difficult. There's nothing wrong with doing the easy things first.

If it is important to you to develop physically but you don't exercise or work out, then obviously you need to remove that liability by starting an exercise program. If one of your objectives is to develop intellectually but you waste time watching television, then you should remove that liability by cutting back on TV and spending more time in intellectual pursuits such as reading or developing your public-speaking ability. If you have trouble controlling your feelings, then one solution would be to consult with a professional or obtain books by recognized authorities on the subject. If you feel uncomfortable around people and in social environments, you might sit down with two or three people and talk about nonwork or nonprofessional things in a social setting and then evaluate the session afterward.

Below are concrete examples of assets and liabilities written by elite performers, among the best in the world. Some of them are from the corporate environment and some are from the world of sport. Look at the lists. You will see that they are no different from many of the things you would list for your own assets and liabilities. You will also see how, in many cases, assets and liabilities are matters of degree:

SAMPLES FROM ELITE PERFORMERS

ASSETS:	LIABILITIES:
Want to win	Complacency
Size	Too intense
Strength	Dwell on the negative
Love of game	Lack of quickness
Open-minded	Fearful
Intelligent	Think too much
Good money manager	Intimidated
Talented	Lack of patience
Respected by peers	Perfectionist
Good values	Stubborn
Generous	Quick-tempered
Great family	Intolerant
Good support system	Poor stress management
Personable	Too emotional

If you do not understand what assets you have, it will be very difficult for you to wake up every morning expecting to win. In fact, it frequently does not matter how good you feel, if you cannot perform as you desire to perform. No matter how well you're able to visualize success, you must possess the assets to execute and accomplish.

YOU MUST BE SPECIFIC

That is why you must be specific, meticulous and committed to identifying your assets and your liabilities. If you do so, the topics in the following chapters will be much easier for you to understand and to have confidence in using them to win every day.

There are two worksheets at the end of this chapter. One is for you to list your assets and liabilities. After you have done this, share the lists with others whom you know, personally and professionally. Ask them to do the same. You will discover that this will give you a better understanding of where you are and where you want to go. The liability side especially will determine where you want to go.

IMPORTANT! ON THE WORKSHEET THAT FOLLOWS:

1. List your assets in no order of priority but just as you think of them. Do not look for a specific number. Whether you have two or 20 will not determine your potential for success.

2. List your liabilities, again in no order of importance.

3. Develop an action for each liability, either to make it an asset or to eliminate it. Each action must be specific, time-oriented and attainable.

4. List an action for each asset as a means of maintaining that asset. This is CRITICAL. You must protect your assets while you deal with your liabilities!

5. Share your lists with those who are important to you personally and professionally.

6. Have others on your team (your family, your job, etc.) go through the same process.

ASSETS AND LIABILITIES
(LIST IN NO ORDER OF PRIORITY)

ASSETS:

1.

2.

3.

4.

5.

6.

7.

8.

9.

10.

ASSETS AND LIABILITIES
(LIST IN NO ORDER OF PRIORITY)

LIABILITIES:

1.

2.

3.

4.

5.

6.

7.

8.

9.

10.

KEY 2

Bucking the System — Expecting to Win

EXPECTATIONS CONTROL WHAT YOU ACHIEVE

This chapter has special significance for me. It covers principles that have had a lasting impact on my life, personally and professionally. The reason is very simple: Expectations influence, and even determine, what you achieve. It makes no difference what assets and liabilities you have, what your goals are or what talents you possess — if you hold negative expectations about yourself, it will be very difficult for you to win. It's like trying to not miss a free throw in basketball. It's a misconception to think that if you can avoid failure then you are sure to succeed. Why? Because there is usually only one or two ways to do something correctly — but there are hundreds of ways to do things incorrectly.

It is frustrating in my professional life to see people content with surviving without the positive expectations that would make them winners. They can do "okay" in a lot of environments. They can be risk free. They can, in their minds, be competitors. They can avoid devastating defeats. But too many times in these same environments that tolerate and support the survivors, if you have more positive expectations and are willing to verbalize them, you are put down because you set a higher standard, a standard that carries increased accountability and higher expectations. You will find that a lot of people resent others who have strongly positive expectations. They would rather survive, a less than fulfilling way of life, but some people are happy living that way.

On the other hand, if you expect to win, you at least increase the probability in your favor. Positive expectations are the key to winning. But they present a tough hurdle, probably the toughest to leap simply because in our culture we are trained from birth to respond to negative expectations. Think about any environment, from preschool to the home to the office, and it is easy to find plenty of people with negative expectations, or, at the least, without positive expectations. There are many people who don't have to win to maintain an average level of achievement and success. This mindset is equivalent to negative expectations.

The process of creating this mindset begins early in life. About the time a baby can focus on Mommy's face, the parents start saying, "No," and keep it up steadily from then on. As the baby adapts to the crib, the parents are saying, "Don't lie on your back," "Don't lie on your side," "Don't knock the mobile down." The negatives become a habit.

Then the kids reach four and five years of age, and they go out for T-ball, the earliest stage of baseball. If you have never had the opportunity to watch a T-ball game and hear a coach talk to his little players, you should do this at least once. You'll hear the coach tell the kids: "If they hit it to you, don't miss," "If you catch it, don't throw it to the wrong base," "If you hit it, don't run the wrong way." And the parents sit in the stands and say, "Don't embarrass us." It is very difficult for the kids to think about succeeding because they spend most of their time trying not to fail in order to please those in authority. And some T-ball coaches actually mete out punishment to their four- and five-year-old players. I have seen a coach pick up a kid who struck out and physically throw the boy over the fence and yell, "Don't come back!" I have seen a coach make a little kid who struck out get down in front of the whole crowd — his team, the opposing team, the parents in the stands — and do 15 pushups, a form of Marine Corps discipline for a five-year-old child who thought he was supposed to be having fun. It is one of the worst forms of attaching expectations to punishment.

NEGATIVE EXPECTATIONS INHIBIT WINNING

Expectations should be attached to becoming successful. The attachment of punishment is the primary reason we grow up with negative expectations and respond better to negative reinforcement in the short term, programmed to avoid failure and rarely expected to succeed. This leads to avoiding failure, assuming success will be a natural result. But it does not follow.

None of the negative reinforcements in T-ball made sense to me. So I signed up to coach T-ball with the goal of giving kids a fun-filled experience so they would continue to play year after year and learn skills along the way, then make a good decision when they were 13 or 14 about whether they wanted to play baseball. My aim was for them not to quit T-ball because of their negative experiences. If they walked away, it would be for the right reasons, and in fact that's what they did.

Realizing that we begin to say "no" to kids when they are very young infants and that by the time they reach 18 years old, they have been told over 185,000 times what not to do, I set out to create a positive environment. Every practice I had a ball for every player and his or her parent. I made sure that everyone was on the field playing as much as possible. In addition to helping the youngsters work on their basic skills, my underlying motive was to get parents involved so that they would spend time throwing and catching with their kids in their own backyards.

Coaching T-ball was a rewarding experience. Many of those kids have stayed in baseball. Many have gone to other sports and used the same principles that we taught, learning basic skills, having fun in the process, expecting to do well and playing to win every single day because of positive expectations.

You'll find the same phenomenon in the educational environment — negative expectations everywhere in the physical setting and the teaching itself. How many times do you see children criticized for what they do wrong rather than congratulated for what they do right? Once again, the result is that children spend most of their time trying to avoid the small percentage of negative events instead of focusing on their assets, magnifying them and flaunting them. They keep trying not to fail, and they grow up that way. The cumulative effect is tremendous. By the time children are 18 years old, they've been told what *not* to do more than they have been told what they should — or *could* — do. Is it any wonder they grow up responding better to negative expectations or to negative reinforcements than to positive input?

Negative expectations abound in higher education and continue in the workplace. Whenever an executive stands up in front of his associates and says, "Let's survive the shakeout," he sets up negative expectations. He is saying, "We're not going anywhere. We're going to just try to survive. We're hoping to be around when the smoke clears." But many of those companies are not around for the same discussions a year later. They are not around because nobody tried to win. Nobody wanted to take risks. Nobody wanted to be visible. They just wanted to avoid failure.

Because negative expectations permeate the environment, you must have an attitudinal upheaval before your assets or your talents will help you to win. You have to expect good things to happen and you must open the emotional doors so that good things can come in. It is extremely important that you *genuinely want to expect* good things to happen. Then you must be totally committed to making good things happen. But you must be committed on a full-time basis. The issue is not whether people have positive expectations each morning. If I ask a thousand people in an audience, "How many of you have positive expectations every day?" the overwhelming majority would raise their hands. The problem is the people who have positive expectations in the morning but after one o'clock in the afternoon just expect to be breathing for the rest of the day, or the people who work the first half of the day to win and the second half to just survive. Do the math, and it means you are devoting two and one-half days a week to winning and two and one-half days to avoiding failure. That is not good enough. The solution requires what I call a major attitudinal upheaval regarding expectations.

NEGATIVE EXPECTATIONS ARE PERVASIVE

Negative expectations surface everywhere. Recently I was on a flight where the flight attendant did an exceptionally good job. As I was leaving the aircraft I told him that I wanted to talk to him for a minute, and then I asked for his name. My intention was to write the airline a letter commending the flight attendant. But he didn't know this, and he became very nervous and embarrassed. "What did I do wrong?" he asked. In the workplace, when you tell someone, "I want to see you in my office in five minutes," how many times does that person think, "Wow! I'm going to get a raise! He's going to tell me what a good job I'm doing!"

To the contrary, most of the time the person will immediately start thinking, "What did I do wrong?" Think of how you'd react if you got a call at home and were told, "It's your supervisor. He wants to talk to you right now." Would you say, "Tell him I'm not in" because you wanted to prepare for what might be the worst? It's a situation that gives most people high anxiety.

In fact, the corporate environment often conveys the same negative atmosphere. When the executive leaves the office and starts walking down the hall, the first perception of employees may be that he is looking for problems, checking for mistakes, trying to catch somebody idle or making a personal call. In fact, the executive may be looking for positive things. Even if he isn't, I think that increasing positive expectations within the workplace might cause him to change his attitude. Positive reinforcement — building expectations to win — must be cultivated, it must be restored to a dominant place in our culture.

EXPECTATIONS ARE INTERNAL AND EXTERNAL

It is significant that when people are asked why they left their jobs at various companies their reasons often have very little to do with money or position. Many times, the primary factor is that they did not know what was expected of them. It is virtually impossible to hold positive expectations if you don't know what is expected of you, which involves both external and internal expectations — what you expect of yourself and what others expect of you.

The external expectations may be entirely different from the internal ones. How many times has someone on the job told a manager, who was upset about something not done or done improperly, "But I thought you wanted me to do this," or "I thought you wanted it done this way." In analyzing your own expectations regarding your work environment, it is a good idea to find out what others expect of you before you write down your internal expectations. If you are to be successful on your job, there must be consistency between what your employer expects of you and what you believe you can bring to the job.

FEAR OF FAILURE AND FEAR OF SUCCESS

The fear of failure undoubtedly is present in everyone's daily life. It is not necessarily a negative quality. Fear of failure, up to a certain point, can be an incentive to perform better. When it reaches or crosses that point, the fear of failure becomes an inhibiting and paralyzing inner force that creates a strong detriment to performance.

Fear-of-failure people are easy to spot because they usually choose one of two directions. They either accept projects that no one else could do, and if they fail, it's no big deal because no one could do the project anyway; or, they accept projects in which they can succeed if they're breathing and walking, projects so easy that failure is not an option.

Fear of failure is relatively easy to overcome. You only need to identify what causes the fear, then develop actions to deal with those inhibitors. A plan of specific actions, at scheduled times, is essential. Then you are placed in situations where you can succeed. In other words, negative expectations can be reversed by persuading yourself that you are good at something and then putting yourself in situations where you can flaunt those assets. Then as you begin to experience success, you can tackle more difficult challenges, and eventually success becomes the rule rather than the exception in your life. You become a winner, not just a survivor.

I worked with a pitcher who had a fear of failure because he was constantly thinking about his liabilities — his change-up and his slider. His fastball was a tremendous asset. We did two things. First, we watched videotapes of his games and focused on the sliders and change-ups that were strikes. This convinced him that he could throw these two pitches.

Second, he learned to throw those pitches more strategically, in situations that would not hurt him. He became a successful three-pitch pitcher.

In business, you simply schedule your "numbers" meetings in the mornings and your "strategic" discussions in the afternoons, accommodating the cyclical nature of your central nervous system. This simple scheduling process can eliminate negative expectations.

Simply stated, when you begin to taste success, you succeed more often.

Fear of success is a syndrome much more difficult to remedy. This is true because fear-of-success people are what I call "rally and fall-back people." Here is why: When I sit down and talk with them about why they are not more successful and what they can do to perform at a higher level, they buy into the program. They become more successful all of a sudden. Of course, this results in higher expectations and increased accountability in their environment. They become more visible. The need to take more risks also increases. At that point, most of these fear-of-success people become very uncomfortable and fall back rather than move ahead. They sit down with me again for a session. Then they rally again. Then they fall back again.

Their mindset is similar to tennis team players who are content to stay number two or three behind the top player who gets most of the visibility and tries to meet higher expectations. These second- and third-place players can win at that level and become comfortable there — even though they probably have the talent to challenge for the number-one spot. The same thing happens on golf teams. Players may have the abilities to perform at a much higher level but they do not.

There is real danger in falling victim to low expectations of yourself and others. This was driven home to me in an unlikely environment — a state home for mentally deficient children in the early 1970s, where I had the privilege of spending several months with children, many of whom had been diagnosed at the time as educable mentally retarded (EMR) with IQs around 80.

One of the youngsters stood out. Although his IQ was in the range of the other children, something about him did not fit with that environment. In checking the records of the children there, I discovered that this child while in elementary school had been very bright, but, as a result of the slow pace of his classmates, he became bored. He probably was intimidating to his teachers. He did not fit the mold. He didn't put his head on his desk when he finished his assignments. He wanted more. Teachers were uncomfortable with that; in fact, they were intimidated by this very bright, creative kid. He also intimidated his parents, who were illiterate and had no idea how to deal with him. By some strange process, the child ended up in this state facility where most of the children were classified as EMR.

When the boy was first admitted, his IQ tested at around 120. He soon became very unpopular with the other children because he could read a book while they were reading a page. He could get dressed and be outside while they were still lacing their shoes. He did things the others could not do and did them very efficiently. Consequently, he was very unpopular. But he was also very perceptive. Having a strong — and perfectly natural — need to belong, to be part of a group, and to be accepted, he quickly figured out what he needed to do in this environment in order to make the best of it. So within eight to nine months, he was taking hours to read one page and taking a long time to dress himself and to do everything else. He became completely consistent with the behavior around him — and when he took the group IQ test, his score was down to 80. His story is a stunning testimony to how important being a part of a group is to anyone, especially children, and how important it is to be accepted by their peers.

The boy with the 120 IQ, after less than a year, came to the point where he did not expect to perform well. But by performing as expected, he found acceptance, and he became content where he was. It is, admittedly, an extreme case, but it illustrates the rule that when little or nothing is expected, little or nothing will be accomplished. If a person is placed in a nonlearning, nonstimulating and depressing environment, then negative expectations become the rule. When you have the talent and the assets, it is the expectations, internally and externally, that separate you from others with equivalent talents and assets.

POSITIVE EXPECTATIONS: THE WINNING ATTITUDE

Positive expectations are necessary as a supplement to whatever product or service we have to offer. Selling revolves around expectations. A sale may be closed or lost when the salesperson enters the prospect's office and before any product is placed on the table. How that salesperson carries himself and projects himself, the expectations he has — these are critical in conveying a positive expectation, a winning attitude. If an executive calls a staff meeting with the expectation that it will be a waste of time, he carries and projects that negative expectation to the group. The result: a negative meeting.

That is what happens in some of those meetings on the mound in professional baseball.

Too many times I have listened to pitching coaches talk to pitchers. It absolutely makes me cringe to hear the coach say, "Whatever you do, don't walk this guy," or "Whatever you do, don't throw inside," or "Whatever you do, don't throw a high fastball." Then the coach walks off the mound, leaving open what the pitcher is supposed to do.

The fact is that the pitcher already knows what he is supposed to avoid doing. There probably are a hundred wrong things he could do and only one or two right things in a given situation. Rather than telling the pitcher, "Don't throw inside," if the coach wants the pitch low and outside, then he ought to say, "Throw this guy low and outside." But trying to get high-level performers to avoid failure assuming they are going to be successful at it just doesn't work most of the time.

It is a paradox that the higher-performing people often seem to be more fragile emotionally. Keep this in mind when you are communicating with others, whether you are a parent talking with your child or an executive in a business meeting or an athlete in a sport environment. It takes years to build a positive self-concept. *It takes a 10-second comment to wreck it.*

It's not good enough that we personally have positive expectations. We simply have to do everything we can within our environment to create the same expectations in everyone else involved, positive expectations that enable people to do their jobs better, to keep people from overworking, to enable them to perform well. Most of these outcomes depend upon expectations.

Expectations cause us to be what we are. This truth is at the core of learning how to be a winner instead of a survivor.

A professional golfer had failed to qualify for his Professional Golfers Association tour card that would allow him to take part in the pro tour for several years. He failed because of his low expectations. This young athlete understood what he wanted to do and where he wanted to go — and what he needed to do to get there. His problem was his own assessment of his capabilities, and that was not a physical issue. He simply *did not expect* to be as good as other players, and he had the perception that everybody was watching his swing and evaluating him, which is a natural phase that young golfers go through. He didn't realize what he was capable of doing and how he could mentally supplement his physical talents.

Together he and I analyzed what he was doing and dealt with focusing and mental recovery techniques. He learned to recover quickly after hitting a bad shot. He learned to store good shots mentally, to build up a repertoire of good shots that he could call on whenever he needed them. We discussed goals and attached performance to the goals. He went on to become a great golfer — winning, not surviving.

Self-doubt appears most active in people with negative expectations. This trait asserts itself when things are not going well, when you don't expect to be successful. It comes into play with some of the best performers in the sports world.

Why would a top catcher in pro baseball be unable to throw the ball back to the pitcher? Why would a third baseman be unable to throw the ball to first? Or why would a hitter not be able to hit left-handers? All have one trait in common: negative expectations for executing the skill involved. The infielder can't throw to first base — because he thinks he can't. The catcher can't get the ball back to the mound — because he doubts himself. The hitter can't hit left-handers — because he does not believe he can hit left-handers.

If I could talk with every child, this is what I would say: "We expect good things from you. We expect you to be successful." Then I would place every child in a positive environment at home, at school where their classrooms would project positive expectations, and in all other environments. I would teach and coach them with positive expectations from the day they entered the world. There is no question that the children would achieve success and that they would grow up to be adults expecting to do well.

Expectations make the difference. It doesn't matter what you do. If you prepare French fries in a fast-food restaurant, expect to be the very best at preparing those fries. If you're a teacher, expect to be the very best teacher at your level. If you're a race car driver, expect to be the very best — expect to win. If you're a pitcher, expect to throw strikes. If you're a hitter, expect to hit the ball. If you're a basketball player, expect to make your shots. If you have positive expectations, your probability of success is far greater than it is if you are only expecting not to fail and trying not to make mistakes.

This is not guesswork. It is proven fact. Over and over and over again, I have seen the results, sometimes dramatic results, of a person expecting to win. Without exception, positive expectations have turned people's lives around. They will do the same for you.

Buck the system — and expect to win.

EXPECTATIONS

**USE THIS WORKSHEET FOR LISTING
EXPECTATIONS TO HELP YOU WIN EVERY DAY.**

A. LIST 5 SELF-EXPECTATIONS (PERSONALLY)

1.

2.

3.

4.

5.

LIST 5 THINGS OTHERS EXPECT OF ME (PERSONALLY)

1.

2.

3.

4.

5.

EXPECTATIONS
**USE THIS WORKSHEET FOR LISTING
EXPECTATIONS TO HELP YOU WIN EVERY DAY.**

B. LIST 5 SELF-EXPECTATIONS (PROFESSIONALLY)

1.

2.

3.

4.

5.

LIST 5 THINGS OTHERS EXPECT OF ME (PROFESSIONALLY)

1.

2.

3.

4.

5.

KEY 3

Goal-Setting — Doing Better Than "The Best You Can"

"THE BEST YOU CAN" JUSTIFIES SURVIVAL MENTALITY

Do you want to just be a survivor? Then do the "best you can."

Everyone at some point has been told just to "do the best you can." There are mornings when we look outside. If it's a bad day, then we just want to do the "best we can" to get through the day. We go into a meeting in the morning at the office or the plant, and if we don't hear the kind of things that are encouraging, then our mindset is just to do the "best we can."

Athletes fall into this trap when they don't feel good physically or if they don't have a lot of confidence in certain situations. They decide to do "the best" they can. This is painfully obvious, if you're a sports fan, when you see teams that have tremendous talent and athletes who obviously play hard but subconsciously may shut themselves down. Physically, they will tell you, "We're doing the best we can." But subconsciously they hold themselves back. They play hard, but there's often a difference between playing hard and playing to win, just as there is between quality-oriented performance versus quantity-oriented performance.

It's human nature to feel "I'll just do the best I can," but based on my 30 years of working with people to make them winners, it's a very dangerous posture to take when you're trying to succeed at anything, if you are content with the generally accepted concept of doing the best you can. That's saying it is the best you *think* you can do, and in reality, it means any level of performance is acceptable.

ACHIEVEMENT OF GOALS SEPARATES THE WINNERS FROM THE SURVIVORS.

And when you talk about achieving goals, unless those goals are very specific, you don't really have much to hang your hat on.

Specific techniques are necessary for professional athletes as well as nonathletes to establish and reach their goals. Goals demand specific actions. Goals must be designed to elevate performance to the next level or to maintain a high level of performance. There are times when you reach a new level that you want to take a deep breath and enjoy a winning environment. You use goals to maintain where you are, so that you don't lose the winning edge. At most other times you want to use goals to move to a higher level.

BARRIERS TO GOAL ACHIEVEMENT

There are barriers to goal achievement. Understanding these barriers is crucial to your learning to win. Some barriers are under your control, others are not. Barriers can be detrimental or supplemental to your goal achievement. They affect your achievement in almost any situation in life, whether personal or professional. Once the barriers are identified, it gives us a place to start, so that we can begin to control the things that we can control and to try to remove the others (or at least learn to live with them).

By examining some of the more common barriers, you can more easily identify the barriers in your own environment — and deal with them. Following are the same impediments that plague many other corporations, sports teams and individuals:

1. *A breakdown in communications.* This seems to pop up in the top three barriers on every list in any corporate environment and in most sport environments. It includes not listening, or people who claim to listen but do not hear what is said; and not wishing to communicate. It also shows up as *different perceptions of the same thing in the environment.* For example, everyone in the executive office understands the company's policies, but as the policies filter down through the levels of management, by the time they get to the people who are to implement the policies, those people don't understand them. This happens many times with parents, who expect certain things of children and think that they've communicated their expectations only to discover that the children's perceptions are very different.

2. *Lack of teamwork.* In sport environments it appears that nobody on the team is rewarded (at least financially) for teamwork, which is avoided in favor of individual performance. This barrier appears often in sales-oriented environments where salespeople are rewarded for individual performance, not for helping the team win.

3. *Lack of understanding of the team philosophy.* Whether it is a personal team in the family or a professional team in the corporate environment or a sports team, everyone needs to be attached to some type of working philosophy.

4. *Lack of planning.* A common problem is that everyone does a three-year plan or a five-year plan, and then those plans are redone every three and five years, respectively. My question is, "What did you plan to do today? What do you plan to do before noon? What did you plan to do between 1 and 5? And how does that relate to the five-year plan and the three-year plan?"

5. *Lack of firm priorities.* This barrier shows up when you have your priorities set in the morning, and after one phone call, your Number 1 priority becomes Number 4 or 5 on the list. This barrier can be overcome by establishing yourself in an environment in a way that lets other people know what your priorities are, so that they're less willing to interfere with those priorities.

6. *Lack of follow-up.* This is a major barrier in almost every environment. Directions are given and there is no follow-up, not necessarily to check up on people to make sure they're

doing what they're supposed to, but follow-up to reinforce, to compliment, to encourage people to want to do more than what is expected of them.

7. *Fear of rejection.* Everybody, no matter what the environment, wants to be a part of something. We are social beings. Fear of rejection can be a fatal barrier, especially for salespeople. This barrier is removed when you understand that failure is a part of learning and that the losers in sport or business or anywhere else are the people who fail to recover quickly from adversity. The more specific you are in dealing with the fear of rejection, the quicker you are going to be able to recover.

LEARNING TO SET YOUR GOALS

The mechanics of goal setting are relatively simple if they're followed consistently. Do you have goals on Monday but don't remember those goals on Tuesday? You have goals for the year, but when do you look at them? You look at them a month before the year's up if you are typical. You may have quarterly goals. Do you look at them every couple of months or every three months?

You must have something specific that you want to accomplish every single day without fail. That is the critical rule in goal-setting and goal achievement.

It's critical, no matter what you do — if you're in the home, if you're a parent, if you're a student, if you're a professional person. It really makes no difference what you do. *You should have something specific* that you want to accomplish every single day.

When you pick up this book, for example, you should have something specific that you want to get out of it. It gives you some direction. It causes you to keep moving ahead.

Again, setting goals is a simple process. Along with being specific, goals need to be difficult. They need to stretch your system. But they need to be attainable. At the same time, they need to be attached to a timetable or schedule, so that you have some point at which you evaluate what you've done in the time interval that you set down. Doing "the best you can," as defined in this chapter, just doesn't fit any of these criteria.

A few years ago a professional golfer was on the PGA tour, his first year on the tour, and he had worked long and hard to get there. Some golfers go to PGA tour school a dozen times, even 14 times in one case I'm familiar with, and never get to the PGA tour. This particular golfer had tried six times before he made it on the tour. He asked for my help. The first thing we did was to sit down and talk about his goals for that first year. It was very obvious that his goals consisted of not losing his card, which permitted him to make the tour. His goals didn't necessarily relate to winning but they related to putting himself in position to win. He wanted to play in a certain number of tournaments. He had some idea of the scores he wanted to shoot, what he wanted to accomplish with his mechanics as far as driving and putting and so forth.

The golfer did achieve a lot of those goals. The next year we talked about his pushing his goals to the next level. Essentially, this is what I told him:

"The first year, you tried to not lose your card. That's fine. You got comfortable in the environment. You learned to live in that environment, which is very, very difficult for a lot of people, and you've proved you can do that. Your driving distance was good. You've proved you can do that. And you're a great putter." There were many other positive results, but they were well below the level for which that golfer should have been striving, and to let him be content at that lower level would, in effect, result in his developing a "survivor" mentality.

"Now for the next year," I told him, "you want the goals to relate to winning, not only to put yourself in position to win but to in fact win a tournament, to be in the top 30 on the money list." Those goals pointed upward as opposed to pointing downward, and many of those goals were also accomplished. But even the goals that he didn't reach served the purpose of pushing this player so that he stretched his capabilities and learned that he could do things he did not think himself capable of doing in golf at the outset.

Other determinants of goal achievement include the physical environment and the psychological environment. Of course, the physical environment is obviously composed of what surrounds us. The psychological environment consists of what is called psychological noise and distractions, things that tend to interfere with performance. We'll deal with these concepts in more detail when we come to Key 10.

SET APPROPRIATE GOALS

It is psychologically devastating to set your goals so high that in the middle of the year or the middle of the week you have to reset them and scale them down. It is much better to set goals that you can achieve, and then set higher goals. It establishes a better environment and is healthier for you to do that.

The achievement of specific goals must be a natural consequence of hard work. It's appropriate as a lifelong process to understand that you must first establish your goal and then achieve it with a good work ethic. You use your time effectively and efficiently. Once you get comfortable in the environment, then you look to achieve specific things. The young soccer player who runs hard every game for five weeks in that sixth game may try to score a goal, which is very specific. So you have to set yourself up to become comfortable in the environment, which enables you to try to achieve specific goals.

When I was called in to do an all-day seminar for a small company, the sales manager explained the objective this way: "We have a limited product. We have a niche market. We have five sales people. But we have a potentially huge market." The challenge was to bring the sales force to a higher level, a winning level.

The morning of the seminar, the sales manager talked to me before we went into the conference room. He told me not to worry about the young man who would be seated on his left because that salesman was going to be fired.

"I don't want to fire him," the sales manager said. "So I've set his goal at a million dollars so that he will get discouraged and quit."

That was a very inhumane way to treat another person, very disrespectful. I took it on myself to pay particular attention to that young salesman as I did the seminar. I learned that he was the brightest of the group, without question, and that he also had more energy than the other four salespeople put together. But those assets had become liabilities. Why? Because when he was hired, management told him he was so bright and had so much energy it wasn't necessary to spend the time training him. "Just go sell," he was told.

Consequently, without training, the young salesman had no focus at all and no vision for what he wanted to accomplish except to work hard. So I took him aside and we worked hard on improving his approach and changing his mindset. We implemented the program, gave him specific goals, and we worked on a weekly basis. The salesman began to achieve and before the year was out, his sales hit $1.5 million. He accomplished more than he ever imagined he could — and he's getting better every year.

The determining factor in winning may be your talents. It may be someone else's talents. It may be the level of competition. The important thing is for you to fit your talents and your skills to goals that are appropriate so that you can guide yourself along the way. Ask yourself if you have the mechanics to do what it is you wish to achieve, then find out where it is you want to take your skills, where you want to go with them.

Atlanta Braves ace pitcher John Smoltz answered these questions years earlier. When I first started working with John, he had very general goals and very general expectations, many of them negative. We worked toward specific goals, one of which was to throw every pitch to accomplish something — not being distracted by the game as a whole, but focusing on every pitch to accomplish what he wanted to do with it. Another goal was to recover from a bad pitch before he threw the next pitch. Once he had that mindset, he became not only a great pitcher that very season, but he turned his career around and became arguably the most durable pitcher in baseball for nearly a decade.

One of my most unforgettable students was a weightlifter. He came to me before the Olympics one year and said he wanted to become an Olympic weightlifter. It was a worthy goal and relatively specific, but what did he need to do to reach the goal? He needed to achieve certain things in different lifts in different positions.

In weightlifting, the athletes get three chances to lift each weight. My would-be Olympic competitor invariably failed on his first lift and just as often failed on the second lift. Then he could not make the third lift simply because he was trying to not miss again. What he learned was to leave each lift and go to the next lift. If he missed the second lift, then it was gone. He went on to the next lift, looking to achieve, not looking to avoid failure. Consequently, he developed strong mental techniques and went to the Olympics — where he set an impressive record, and he did it on the third lift. He learned to do better than what he thought was the best he could.

A tennis player who made All-America in college couldn't win at the pro level even though he had plenty of talent. And he was playing as hard as he could, as he told me. "I play hard. I do the best I can." Consequently, if he played hard and lost it was okay. If he played hard and won, it was okay. If he competed well, it was okay.

"If you don't play to win, then don't play," I advised him. "If you don't have specific things to accomplish, don't play. That doesn't mean you have to win every match, but if one of the things you want to accomplish is hitting great serves, and you still lose the match, but in your evaluation you realize you did in fact hit great serves — then you won in that area. If you wanted to hit good backhands, and you hit good backhands — then you won in that area.

"You break your goals down into every part of your game so you can take the positive things to the next match. If you lost a match because you did certain things poorly but you served well, then take the good serves to the next match, and set your goals to hit better groundstrokes or play at the net better."

Using the keys to winning, that tennis player, who ranked below nearly 300 others in world standings, climbed into the top 30 and performed in Davis Cup competition.

It wasn't magic, and it's not meant to be portrayed as magic. It was very simply that he learned to supplement his physical talent with a positive mindset facilitated and driven by setting specific goals. Go into any environment and you will find that to be true — in the corporate environment, in the home, and personally, whether the goal is to become a better employee, a better spouse, a better teacher or a better student.

SHARE AND UNDERSTAND YOUR GOALS

A critical aspect of goal-setting is that you must share your goals with other people in a very specific way so that everybody understands the meanings of the goals. Put them in writing. People can't have different perceptions of what you put on paper. Everybody has to see the same thing. That is one of the reasons goals must be very specific.

Failure to do this can be very costly. At a corporation I worked with to cut costs and improve efficiency, the cost-control goals were passed down from the executive level to the plant workers. But something was lost in the translation, at least with respect to one of the workers. He was assigned to secure a lid left off one of the drums containing waste in the warehouse. Securing the lid would have taken about two minutes and cost about $10 in labor. Instead, the worker decided to change the lid, and he left the drum open as he went off to look for a new one. En route, he encountered his supervisor, who told him to go to another location and move a forklift. In the meantime, a federal inspector came by, saw the open drum and fined the company $100,000.

Had the worker and his supervisor understood clearly how every cost-control measure related to everything they did, the outcome would have been different. Too often, people take for granted that all those involved have a clear understanding of the goals.

It is critical that you, and everyone associated with you, personally or professionally, understands what your goals are and what you need to do to reach them.

YOUR GOALS MUST BE SPECIFIC

List your goals for the next 12 months. Then review them and break them down into subgoals, or smaller parts of each goal. This makes clear and specific what you plan to do. The importance of writing down your goals cannot be overemphasized.

Take the case of a professional baseball player, who decided to quit the game and walk away from baseball in the middle of spring training. This player had a mindset problem. He looked at the end of the season in October and worried about his performance not being good enough for the kind of season he wanted. He was unable to see anything in March that related to the statistics he hoped to have in October. Those statistics appeared impossible to achieve.

We went to dinner, and at the restaurant I asked the waitress to bring us a stack of paper napkins. "Okay," I said to the baseball player. "If you're going to walk away, let's talk about what you would have wanted to accomplish by October if you had stayed."

The player described his goals for the end of the year. Then I asked him what he would have wanted to accomplish by the All-Star break in mid-July. Then we moved the date back to May, then April, all the time writing down specific goals for each month and relating them to October.

"What would you want to accomplish by April 1 opening day?" I asked. We wrote down those goals. This was on March 12, and there was a game the next day.

"Just for discussion," I said, "what would you want to accomplish tomorrow relating to those goals — during the game? Then let's break those down to what happens during the game and what you would want to accomplish with each at-bat. Then let's break that down. What would you want to accomplish with each pitch at each at-bat?"

Next we related all those goals to October. We took the first pitch of the next day's game and related that to the October goals. Once he had written down his goals, then broke them down into daily doable parts, his mindset and his performance changed dramatically. During the season, we checked his goals against his performance day by day, week by week and then month by month. It got to be fun looking at how he was reaching his goals.

The result was that the player decided to stay — and went on to put up the best record of his career in every offensive category. From then on, he was a top performer for his team. It happened because he took the time to set goals, to work through them, refine them, break them down into doable parts, and then work hard to achieve them.

Will you personally make the decision to look at a specific goal every single morning — maybe not all of them, but one specific goal every morning — for the rest of your life? Right now, at this moment, what do you want to have accomplished at the end of today, whatever this day is?

There must be something specific that you can hold onto, something you can accomplish this day. Not tomorrow. Not next week. Not next month. But today! That is absolutely essential to doing better than the "best you can."

YOUR GOALS MUST GO BEYOND "BEING BETTER"

One of the most dangerous postures to assume is that you just want to be better than other people. That is a road to mediocrity and survival only. Being better than other people does not make you a winner. Being better than other people does not make you great at what you do. It only makes you better than other people with whom you compare yourself. This fact is vitally important to you if you are in a competitive environment, especially in a corporate environment. Having a goal to be the best of 50 salespeople doesn't mean anything — because if they're all poor salespeople, being number one only makes you just a little better than the others. It doesn't make you a winner.

On one of my constant trips via commercial airlines, bag lunches were handed to the passengers on boarding the jetliner. After we were seated, I was amazed when a voice came over the speaker saying, "I need to make an announcement. Those lunches are not for this flight. We don't know how long they've been there. So you might want to sniff the meat and eat that sandwich at your own risk."

Call it absurd, stupid, whatever. But that announcement was made twice. It upset me and even embarrassed me for the airline. I wanted to tell somebody how I felt about it, so I turned to the guy next to me.

"You know, there had to be a better way to do that," I said. "Maybe take an empty trash bag and collect the sandwiches and tell everybody, 'We're sorry. We'll get you free drinks or something.' But don't tell people, 'We messed up.' Don't announce it to the world."

To my surprise, the guy became very defensive. He got right up in my face. "I work for this airline," he told me, "and we're certainly better than the others."

That made absolutely no sense to me. I said to the guy, "Does that make you good?"

If you don't want to use all your assets to become better, if you don't expect to win, if you don't have specific things you want to achieve, if you're not in it to play to win every day — then you probably should just not play the game. If you're just trying to be better than other people, you're not necessarily going to be very good. And you're going to learn to feel good about being better than a very average group.

If you just want to be better than your colleagues, then that's all you'll ever be. And if they get worse every year, you'll continue to be better than that but you'll also get worse. On the other hand, if you have specific things to accomplish and specific actions you want to do, and you stick to your list, then you'll move ahead and you'll separate yourself from the pack. Specific daily goals keep you on the right track and keep you moving forward.

Consider again that golfer who spent his first year on the tour trying not to lose his card, staying ahead of those below the magic number. He kept his card, just barely. The next year he began to focus on winning, on looking up instead of down, and he won more than $500,000. In his third year on the tour, he has won well over $1 million with nine tournaments remaining.

That golfer learned that setting and achieving specific goals can be incredibly fulfilling. You achieve what is called self-actualization — fulfillment — from achieving specific goals that you set out to reach. And that's where you need to be, to understand why you do what you do.

YOU MUST REWARD YOURSELF

Many people achieve their goals, but then they look ahead and see all the goals remaining. All they can think is, "There's still so much to do," and they never realize any benefits from achieving smaller goals along the way.

You must reward yourself. If you set out to achieve something this week and on Friday it's evident that you achieved it, don't look back and say, "Well, I achieved that this week, but there's so much to do for the rest of the month." Reward yourself for this week. Go out to dinner. Do something to reward yourself for having achieved a goal this week. The rewards attach you to the goals. That's what keeps you moving ahead. That's what keeps you going. Keep track of your successes and your wins, not your failures.

If you play golf — those of you who, like me, are not very good golfers — dwell on what you accomplish. If you go out and play 18 holes and you hit 90 shots, obviously, that's not the score you wanted. But if you hit two or three good shots, if you have the mindset I have, then that's enough to make you want to go back and play again.

Some golfers spend all their time worrying about the 47 or the 45 shots they didn't hit well. I look at golf entirely differently. Realizing there are only two or three perfect shots by professionals, I feel good when I hit a couple of good shots. I figure if I go back, I may hit four good shots or I may hit six good shots. But I try to keep moving ahead so that I feel I'm achieving something. And when I do achieve something, I reward myself for that.

SET GOALS FOR EVERYDAY LIFE

There's a major misconception that goals only relate to work.

Goals relate to everything. Goals relate to everyday life. Goals relate to being able to sustain energy, for example, to accomplish what you need to do. You should have goals relating to nutrition, what and how much you eat; goals relating to rest, how much rest you need, how much rest you get; goals relating to exercise, leisure pursuits, time off, and downtime.

Again, the goals must be very specific. Example: "I'm going to get more rest." That doesn't mean anything. But if you decide, "I'm going to get eight hours of sleep every night," that means something. "I'm going to exercise three times a week." That means something but not enough. "I'm going to exercise three times a week for 30 minutes each time." That means more but still not enough. "I'm going to exercise three times a week 30 minutes a day and I'm going to walk 20 minutes on the treadmill and do 10 minutes on the exercise equipment." That's specific. That's something to which you relate, something you hang your hat on. That's something for which you can reward yourself.

Set specific goals for your leisure time and pursuits. "I'll take more time off" doesn't mean anything. "I'll take more time off to spend with family" means more. "To spend time with family and take two vacations a year" means still more. "To spend time with family and take two vacations a year and do specific things on trips with family" is closer to what you need to do.

Goal-setting is not a cumbersome chore, and it shouldn't be perceived as that. It's a very, very easy route to take if you just spend a little time and get into a routine of doing it.

At the end of this chapter there's a worksheet that deals with goal setting, enabling you to set three or four major goals and then break those down to subgoals. And if you want to expand them and break them down even further, do it. The list is there to get you started, so you understand exactly what I'm talking about when I say specific, difficult but attainable, time-oriented goal achievement.

Once you do your goal-setting, you will begin to achieve things that you want to do. You might not achieve them all, but again, as with expectations, what you're trying to do is increase the probability of success. If you don't set any goals, you achieve nothing. If you set 10 goals and achieve eight, then that's eight more things than you would have achieved otherwise. Goals are simply another directional tool to help you become what you would like to be personally and professionally.

Learn to recognize the barriers to goal achievement and control them or climb over them. Set your goals high, long-range and short-range, for the year, the quarter, the month, and without fail for each day that you live. That is how you use the key of doing better than the best you can and winning, not surviving, every day!

GOALS FOR WINNING
FOR EVERY LONG-TERM GOAL, LIST RELATED
SHORT-TERM GOALS. EACH STATEMENT MUST BE
SPECIFIC, AND EACH GOAL MUST BE DIFFICULT BUT
ATTAINABLE WITHIN THE STATED TIME FRAME.

<u>GOAL</u> A:

    A-1

    A-2

    A-3

<u>GOAL</u> B:

    B-1

    B-2

    B-3

GOAL C:

    C-1

    C-2

    C-3

GOAL D:

    D-1

    D-2

    D-3

GOAL E:

    E-1

    E-2

    E-3

KEY 4

Define Your Team: Surround Yourself with Good People

UNDERSTAND YOUR ROLE ON THE TEAM

Winners recognize the importance of the team concept. They know they need to be members of a team, to support the team, and to be supported by the team. They know where they fit in the team. They understand their roles on the team.

The biggest barrier to recognizing or realizing the value of a team is confusion about role definition or a lack of role definition — just what it is a team member is supposed to do. Again, the reason most people give for leaving a company is that they don't know what is expected — that is, they don't know or understand their roles.

As you define your team for winning every day, personally or professionally, you need to decide if you are the point guard or the shooter, to use a basketball analogy. Then you need other team members who complement and support your talents.

This is crucial to the team's success and therefore to your success. If your team has only point guards, and all you do is pass the ball around, then the team never scores. If your team has only shooters, there's nobody to throw the ball in. So you lose either way. On your team, you need leaders and supporters. You need people who are going to take risks and people who are going to support the risk takers. Sometimes you have to do both. You may need to be a utility player, who is able to play more than one role and to play different roles well, to be comfortable in them as a supporter. This is especially true of your professional team, in the corporate environment, but it is also valid in your personal environment.

Sports dramatically illustrate role definition and what happens when team members either don't know or don't accept their roles. A pro baseball team traded for a perennial All-Star player, a Gold Glove winner who had been the star on his previous team. With his new team, he was expected to play less of a leading role and more of a supporting role. He still played. He still did all the things he had done before, but it was clear that he was cast in the role of supporting other players who held the leading positions. This player did not want that role. He did not accept it. Consequently, he did not play well at all, and the team did not play as well as it should have. The reason is obvious: bringing in a player who did not accept his role had a detrimental effect on the team chemistry — how the members related to each other. After one year, the player who did not accept his role was traded to another team. He again became an All-Star and won another Gold Glove. This scenario is not unusual in sports.

The consummate sports team at one time was the Boston Celtics of pro basketball. Everyone involved, from the players to the ushers in the stands to the equipment staff and the front office, bought into the team concept. And while other teams brought in superstars and created excitement, they never really won like the Celtics. They had talent but they had more — a commitment to the team and to talent that fit their team. That is the ideal for your team, personally and professionally.

Probably the ultimate team model in the '90s was shared by the Atlanta Braves and the New York Yankees. The Braves won every division title from 1991 through 1999, a professional baseball record, including five National League championships and one World Series title. The Yankees won more than 400 games from 1996 through 1999, including three World Series championships. Both teams, obviously, have great talent, but there is more to their success than raw talent. They both have a manager who "lets the players play." He relates his expectations to them individually and as a team. Then he creates an environment in which they can, as a team, achieve those expectations. In my judgment, a large measure of their success comes from understanding the team concept — that it takes everyone playing to win for the team to be successful. Every player understands that his role is absolutely vital to the team.

In business, every employee must feel not just important but critical to the team's performance or to the productivity of the team. Every player needs something to which he or she can be attached personally, something to which he or she can make a genuine contribution. In sports, every player must feel critical to the outcome of the game or to the team's status as a winner. In the family, parents must feel critical to the development of their children.

EVERYTHING MUST BE A TEAM EFFORT

Everything we do is basically a team effort. Even in individual sports, there is always a team involved. There is always a support system. There is always someone who understands the goals and the desired outcomes, and then tries to contribute to achieving those goals and attaining the outcomes. You don't always see the other team members, especially in golf. Team building first, followed by teamwork, is an essential concept for winning both personally and professionally.

One of the most detrimental practices to team play in sports is the practice of rewarding players based on individual performance. The reward apparently is not perceived as being based on contributions to the team. Individual players are rewarded, and then the managers and owners hope those individuals will contribute to the team. I see that as a risky way to set up a team. A basketball team can have five great shooters and still lose most of its games. A baseball team can have a roster full of great hitters and still lose most of its games if it doesn't have strong pitching and a good defense to keep the other team from scoring a lot of runs also. For a team to work well, it must have the players who perform the necessary roles.

For your team, you first need to identify and to understand what you want to accomplish and whether or not a team is important to achieving your goals. Then you must determine what members your team needs and the role of each person on your team, personally and/or professionally, and the expectations and accountability of the members and the team.

The process of forming your team requires you to:

1. Evaluate the team goals.

2. Review your assets and liabilities.

3. Determine team talents needed.

4. Select additional team members with needed assets.

Here is an example of a professional golfer going through the process of bringing together his team:

1. Goals are to win a tournament and to be in the top 30 on the money list.

2. Assets needed are: Golf skills, health, stamina, a clear and focused mind, balance, support emotionally and physically. Golfer assets: Elite talent level, commitment, achievement motivated.

3. Team assets needed: Coaching, training, nutrition, family support.

4. Additional team players needed are: a) Coach for mechanics;

b) physical trainer; c) nutritionist; d) family, friends; e) mental development coach.

The critical factor is that the team function properly. Team members participate and contribute at different times, based on the golfer's needs. Of course, all team members must be available when needed.

Teams win and lose, not the individuals who make them up. In order for a team to win, everyone on the team has to make a personal commitment to help the team win. A coach cannot make that happen. Neither can an administrator, or the chairman of the board or a parent. They can create an environment and present the possibilities for the team to achieve. Then they let the people involved make their own decisions about whether or not they genuinely want to be part of a team.

But it only takes one individual on the team to cause it to lose. Have you ever observed a situation where everyone has a good attitude before one negative person walks in — and within 15 minutes the whole team is down? You have to separate yourself and your team from that kind of a "team wrecker." Not having such a person around will automatically improve the probability of your team concept succeeding.

In professional sports, it only takes one person with a negative attitude and negative expectations to cause a team to lose. The manager cannot afford to have those people as part of the team.

Look at National Basketball Association teams, especially those with younger players. I have seen coaches fill their teams with talented young players and then bring in a very talented veteran who did not contribute to the team effort. He became a deterrent to the chemistry of the team, and to the affinity of the players for each other. The attitudes of the younger players were negatively affected. Despite all the talent of those players, that team had a losing record. It happens every time. You can think of teams that experienced it, talented teams with bad chemistry because everyone on the team was not playing for the same thing. Some of the players were playing to not lose. Some were playing for themselves and not the team. Unfortunately, everybody was not playing for the team to win. And it didn't.

The stock car racetrack offers what I believe is the most dramatic example of teamwork and how everyone must pull together to win. The slightest loss of time — a fraction of a second — or a communication failure or a team member's mental lapse — any of these can spell failure. At the start of a Motocross 500 automobile race, I had the good fortune to be in the pit area watching the NASCAR crew. Every member of the crew — the team — had a role to play, and there was total confidence and respect among the members. The crew members performed as a highly organized, highly coordinated team under tremendous stress for hours at a time without a break. The driver pulled into the pit, the crew changed the tires and sent the car screeching onward in mere seconds because the crew members worked as a team, each doing his part to perfection. If one of the members had erred, the teamwork would have been compromised, and the chances of their driver winning could have been seriously diminished.

YOUR TEAM MUST COPE WITH CHANGE

It is amazing how corporate America jumps from buzzword to buzzword looking for the quick fix to greater profits. How many have you heard? There have been "quality circles," "quality management," "excellence," "ownership," "empowerment," "participative management," "team building," "teamwork," and of more recent vintage, "downsizing," "reengineering," and "rightsizing." All are interesting concepts but have been short-lived. They are flash terms. The one thing they do is create change in the environment, sometimes drastic change and sometimes negative change.

What you must put in place when you are forming your team is something enduring. It's going to be there every day. People are going to feel it. People are going to see it. People are going to want to be a part of it. This concept is there when you are gone. It's there if you make changes in your team. It needs to be related to your philosophy of a team, your goals for your team and the foundation of the team. It must be capable of living through even the most dramatic changes in the team. The basic, winning chemistry of the team must still be there, because you still have the same basic philosophy and concept that keep the team's engine running smoothly.

Consider the Atlanta Braves and how they have coped with major changes. The Braves have always taken pride in their team chemistry. They also have talented players, though probably no more talented than some other teams. But year after year, the Braves win. From 1991 through 1999, the Braves won eight straight Eastern Division titles in the National League to set a pro baseball record. But the roster of the 2000 team had only two players left of the 25 who were there in 1991.

The key has been the chemistry, which is a function of the concept. This has been consistent year after year. Players who don't fit the chemistry don't stay long. The Braves from top to bottom have firmly held to the team concept, to the team's foundation and to its goals, never for a moment losing sight of where the organization wants to go.

Change can be exciting and rewarding. Change in a team's makeup can produce marvelous results if it is done for the right reasons and if the goals are kept paramount. In families, you may not have the drastic changes that occur in sports but there are still times that will test your philosophy, your foundation and your goals. But if these basic concepts are what they should be, then you must hold to them, keep them out front, and strive toward those goals every single day without fail. Then you are in the winning mode. However, the people business being what it is, the strongest foundation, the best philosophy, and the most specific goals will not eliminate occasional conflict, another type of change that teams encounter.

In almost every team, whether it is personal or professional, there are going to be conflicts. To be a winning team does not mean that the team members have to love each other. It does mean that they have to respect each other. They have to respect each other's assets and liabilities, and they have to play in a coordinated way. But conflicts are part of the equation, and in many cases they make a team stronger, especially as they are resolved. Conflict can be positive if it causes change and risk-taking, which are good for the team.

There can be unfavorable consequences to conflict.

These include the emergence of leadership that does not represent the majority, tunnel vision and losing sight of original goals. You have to be perceptive enough to understand when conflict is reaching the edge of becoming detrimental. Then you have to prevent it from going over the edge.

EVERYONE ON YOUR TEAM COUNTS

Recognition of the contributions of team members is essential. This is true for every kind of team, whether it is your personal team, your family team, or your corporate team. One of my most enjoyable experiences came when I spoke at a company's annual employee appreciation meeting early in 2000. Every team member, from the cleanup crew to the chairman of the board, attended. Everyone received recognition for his or her contributions to helping the corporate team win — and it was a major winner. All the team members knew each other by name, regardless of their station within the company. Talking with those team members and watching them interact, I could easily see that they shared a strongly coordinated work ethic and common goals. That team had the winning chemistry.

Another meeting provided the reverse image. It was a meeting of nearly 100 partners in a financially related business. All the people attending had offices in the same building in a major city. They had been in that location for nearly 15 years. The youngest had been a partner for about nine years.

My assignment was to speak on team-building. As I sat in the conference room waiting for the meeting to start, I watched people come in and introduce themselves to others.

What a challenge my team-building speech is going to be if the team members don't even know each other, I thought. Where to start? They didn't know each other's assets and liabilities. They didn't know what their expectations and goals were. They knew they wanted to make loads of money.

It is not atypical for that type of business, where people come in, stay a few years, burn out and go out the back door, and others replace them. If that's what they want and they are successful on the bottom line, then they are achieving their goal. But if they want something more fulfilling, then they must make the commitment and expend extraordinary efforts to change their corporate mentality.

BUILDING YOUR TEAM TAKES HARD WORK

How does a team come together? How does it gel? What really makes a group of individuals a team?

One popular approach to team-building is to take people off to the wilderness where they live together for a few days in close quarters, prepare their own food, help each other climb cliffs and do a lot of things that require teamwork. But after they return to their real-life environment, I'm not at all sure that the positive feelings and the teamwork remain after the feel-good wears off.

The truth is that team-building is a very difficult, demanding and ever-changing process. Teamwork is even more difficult to achieve, and it has to be closely attended every single day. Teamwork is not necessarily a consequence of team-building.

There is a rule for team builders, whether corporate

managers, sports managers or parents: You are only as good as the players on your team. As the saying goes: "If the players quit, the coach gets fired." It makes no difference how good the coach is, if the players decided to make him look bad, the coach gets fired. It happens every day in sports and in business.

The answer is for management to provide a philosophy and a common goal, or a set of goals, that can be interpreted and applied to every job or task. You see, even the person who cleans the offices at night needs to understand that he or she is making a critical contribution to the success of the team because those team members are more productive working in a clean environment. Whatever the position or role, it must relate directly to the team and its success.

Team builders must decide what personality they want to show to their constituents and their competitors. Every member of the team has an individual personality, without question. But on winning teams the players are able to incorporate the team personality into their own.

When a company's representative calls on a client, does the client know automatically where that representative is from by the way he or she conducts himself or herself? That needs to happen for the team to win consistently. That is the ideal. It is not a matter of bleeding away an individual's personality. The idea is to supplement that personality with the company's distinct persona. This is even true in sports, where for instance, a Big East conference basketball team is instantly recognizable by its aggressively physical style of playing. Each conference has its own personality.

You should look for team members who fit your team concept. More and more companies perform personality assessments as part of the hiring process. This is driven by the need to know if a new person will fit into the team, what that person brings to the mix. Whatever it is, there is little likelihood the personality traits will change once the person is brought on board.

The most difficult change to achieve in an adult is a behavioral change — to quit smoking or drinking or other habits that have been in place for a long time. Even when the behavior is changed, it is very difficult to sustain the change. So the team-building decision comes down to whether a personality fits, not whether it can be changed. At the same time, each team member needs the freedom to maintain his own identity while supplementing his traits with the team traits.

On your team, you need members who are supporting players. You need others who are independent, others who are venturesome, others who are aggressive risk-takers, and you need other players who want to be in control. To make it the consummate team, you need diversity.

Once the team is assembled, members must understand their team personality. They must understand the team philosophy. They must understand the team's goals and what they mean to each individual player. They need to know what resources are available to reach the goals, and they have to understand what happens when they reach the goals as a team.

Of course, there are many things which must be done every day to ensure the team works properly and successfully. As was emphasized in the opening of this chapter, the role of each member must be clearly defined. Each person must know what is expected of each member.

CORPORATE TEAM-BUILDING:
THE "LEAGUE" CONCEPT

Sometimes in the quest to create a team, especially in business, people lose sight of what makes a team work. Distance, for instance, can defeat a team's effectiveness when the team gets too big or the company is too big to manage. The environment can be stretched so much geographically that it's almost impossible to develop the team feeling or function.

That was the case when I was called in by a major, worldwide corporation for a week's team-building seminar. Nineteen people from 19 different countries attended the seminar in the corporation's New York headquarters. It made no sense that 19 individuals from as many countries could be expected to feel they were part of the corporate team based in New York. Consequently, my presentation shifted from the idea of a team, per se, to the broader concept of a league or a conference.

Since each office in each country had its own individual personalities, each would have its own team. That team developed its goals and philosophy — but each of the 19 teams also had certain goals that fit into the big picture, goals that would make the corporation a winner at the end of the year. It was modeled after a basketball or football conference, where each school had its own individual personality but followed the same guidelines and rules set by the conference.

Corporate management in America needs to understand that regional office personalities can differ — that the personality or culture of a successful New York office is not the same as a New Orleans office or a Los Angeles office, and that it takes different personalities to be successful in those places. Regional teams, combined to form a league, allow people to preserve their identities in such an environment. The objective is to create a highly efficient and effective team.

The league concept accomplishes five things that are vital to a company's success:

1. Competition between the regional or local teams becomes intense, and it drives performance to a higher level.

2. Teams cooperate, in that they try to retain greater performers within their own conference, the company and away from competing companies.

3. Each player feels a special bond to the team when it is an immediate presence, when it's there every day.

4. Players can change teams within the conference and still feel comfortable.

5. Team scores are pooled at the end of the year to produce the conference score, which brings it all together in building a championship corporate spirit.

I worked with a company with five regions in the United States that provided a fascinating illustration of this concept. The rule had been the typical idea of a corporate team: At the annual meeting, management talked about how everyone was part of the team, and for two days there was, in fact, a company team. But then after the meeting ended, the participants returned to their respective offices and, lacking significant communication, no longer felt themselves part of the big team.

This was a league-building opportunity. But a process had to be established in order to ensure the success of the concept. We had to answer these questions:

1. Were the regional managers capable of running a relatively independent team? Could they make critical decisions and be accountable for them — and did they want to be accountable for their team's actions?

2. Were the players serious about being a team within a league? They had to understand the concept and buy into it, totally.

3. Were there clearly established common threads that would hold the team relationship together?

4. Could we massage the conference rules so that each team could flaunt its wares and still play within the rules? Could each team show its individual personality? This was critical.

5. Could the league office communicate with the teams and monitor team performance without running the individual teams? We had to avoid overcontrol from the corporate office, and this was a major challenge because the concept was different from the usual order of things. It was in many respects a decentralization process.

6. Could we establish a league philosophy, a corporate philosophy that could mesh with the regional philosophies? This

would be critical also.

7. Could the league office become a support center for the teams? It would not be an easy task if the corporate office was too wedded to control instead of support.

All these questions ultimately were answered positively, and the teams went to work under the new arrangement. They became stronger and more productive, as did the company as a whole, within a very short time frame. Profits improved — and morale improved significantly in the regional offices.

In an age of corporate trimming or cutbacks, CEOs want greater productivity from fewer employees. This simply means that the energy must be focused on pulling the corporate team together. It's logical, but in the process of reengineering and reorganizing, with the anticipation of pulling the new team together, management fails to recognize that the new team does not feel like a team at all.

To the contrary, many of the individual members feel very alone in the corporate environment, especially after cutbacks. Seen from the top, the perception may be that a strong new team is coming together. But lower down, the perception of the employees, the team members, is that some key players have been cut and now management expects those who are left to play more than one position. Consequently, their individual personalities are diluted. This is a major issue when large companies undergo massive cutbacks in jobs.

It is imperative that top management realize that special attention must be given to the people still on the job, to recognize what each brings to the team, and to assure them of their worth to the team and their part in the future success of the business.

Give people a positive environment in which to work and an immediate group, or team, to which they can belong. Then provide immediate feedback for team performance and individual performance. Add a place where the group can have fun. Mix all these ingredients, and you have high probability of a functioning, successful, winning team.

The whole concept of team-building and teamwork is as critical to your personal life as it is to your professional life. "Team" means you understand how to give and take, how to support, how to lead, how to be a part of something bigger than yourself alone, to belong to a group of individuals working together to achieve, to win, to prove how good they can be at what they do.

Use the worksheets that follow to help you evaluate your personal team structure. Have each team member answer the questions on the second worksheet and then compare notes.

PERSONAL TEAM STRUCTURE

TALENTS/ASSETS NEEDED

1.

2.

3.

4.

5.

6.

PLAYER

1.

2.

3.

4.

5.

6.

PROFESSIONAL TEAM STRUCTURE

TALENTS/ASSETS NEEDED

1.

2.

3.

4.

5.

6.

PLAYER

1.

2.

3.

4.

5.

6.

KNOW YOUR TEAM

WHAT IS EXPECTED OF ME AS A TEAM MEMBER?
WHAT DO I BRING TO THE MIX?

WHAT IS OUR TEAM PERSONALITY?

WHAT ARE THE TEAM'S GOALS AND WHAT
DO THEY MEAN TO ME?

**WHAT RESOURCES ARE AVAILABLE
TO REACH OUR GOALS?**

**WHAT HAPPENS WHEN OUR TEAM
REACHES THE GOALS AS A TEAM?**

KEY 5

Focusing:
Zeroing In on the Target

LOCK IN ON THE CRITICAL THINGS

"Think, think, *think* about what you do!"

How many times have people asked you to think about what you do? Over and over, we hear managers say it to employees. We hear coaches say it to players. We hear parents say it to children. We hear teachers say it to students. We hear teammates say it to each other.

The word "focus" is a popular term, and we hear it a lot nowadays when someone is advising us to think about what we do.

When a coach talks about why a team didn't perform well, somewhere in the conversation "lack of focus" will pop up. When the talk is about becoming better and what a team needs to do to win, without exception the comments are: "We need to focus more. We need to lock in."

These ideas have a positive initial impact, without question. Their effectiveness, however, is short-lived without a definition and understanding of "focus." What exactly does it mean when you say "focus"? Or when you say "think" or "concentrate"? Too many times when the coach tells a team, "We need to concentrate," he then walks away, leaving people wondering, "Concentrate on what?" I've heard coaches say: "That's wrong. We need to concentrate. Let's do it again." The players are wondering, "Do it again, the wrong way?" So you also need to know exactly where to put that focus.

The problem is that coaches and others in charge may stop short of telling people what to do to make their performance better. The effective approach would be to say, "You focused on this. It was incorrect. So you need to change direction and focus on so and so." Until people learn to do that with some consistency, "focus" will be nothing more than a popular, but generic, term.

Focusing has always been a critical part of sports. It's a critical part of business, of raising families, of every phase of your life — if, in fact, you understand what it means so that you can implement focus at any given moment.

THE KEYS TO FOCUSING:

There are two keys to focusing.

1) *Focus on what is to be accomplished rather than on what is to be avoided.*

If we're talking about winning versus surviving, how many people spend a considerable amount of their mental energy focusing on what they want to avoid? In sports, players spend too much time focusing on not missing shots, focusing on not making bad plays. In business, people may be focusing on not losing sales or focusing on not alienating coworkers. In families, parents may be focusing on not having controversy, on not having conflict and not making other family members angry or upset.

As an example, in my program for athletes and even salespeople, we use a lot of videotapes. We videotape people performing, whether pitching or selling. We keep shooting until we get a performance that's considered to be *vintage*, that is, the best we can do. In golf, for example, if I take a professional golfer to the course, and I have him hit 10 drives, and he tells me when we look at those 10 drives on video, "Number five was as good as I can hit a drive," then I throw away the other nine, and I give him a video that consists of probably 15 replays of that one drive. We do other shots the same way. We do short shots. We do putts. We do sand shots. Then we throw away all the shots of flawed performances. We keep only the shots of correct performances for review and study.

When you allow a person to watch an unedited videotape of their performance, the first things they will see are their mistakes. They will look for the flaws, because in order to be successful we have to correct mistakes. I don't argue that point. But when you start picking out all the mistakes, in the process you may miss all the things that you did correctly. Or you may say, "Well, I see some mistakes, but eventually I'll get through it." That's a problem also. If you're focusing on any activity and see something negative in your approach, unless you work your way through it or hop over it and then go to the end, what you've done is store a negative activity. Essentially, you are formulating a plan from your mistakes as opposed to one based on the things you did well before. Any time you attempt that activity again, the negative mindset will control what you do. And your negative file fills up at the expense of your positive one. When you store these negative images, you're taking away from the space that's available for the positive things.

Golfers are especially notorious for focusing on mistakes and trying to come up with the perfect shot. But there probably is no perfect shot. Golfers will complain about their flaws, then conjure up a plan to avoid the flaws. But they don't see the good shots. So it's critical that we throw away the bad shots, that we only show the good shots. If you're going to watch a bad shot, only watch it to make a quick correction, mechanically, then throw that footage away. We discard most of the videotape that is shot.

It is a useless exercise to watch yourself performing incorrectly, no matter what you do. In working with salespeople, it is standard procedure in my program to videotape the presentation, then review it. If we find flaws in the presentation, then we throw it away, and videotape another presentation that eliminates the flaws. When the salespeople replay the presentation, which should be a learning tool, they can focus on what they're able to accomplish instead of what they want to avoid. They learn by watching the correct presentation over and over.

2) *Understand exactly what you are focusing on.*

This requires the ability to define focus. It's not complicated. Focusing is being able to zero in on, or lock in on, only the critical things before and during any activity, whatever that activity might be. Regardless of what you do, you need to focus on something specific. Your focus must be on what you're going to do, again not on what you want to avoid. Always focus on being successful. But to do this you will need to be specific.

A few years ago, a college pitcher at a leading university was a top draft choice by a pro baseball team. In his first year he developed a problem throwing strikes, which is not an unusual problem. The team sent their sports psychologist to work with the rookie. During the process, the psychologist talked at great length about focusing and visualizing. But he didn't know much about baseball.

The young pitcher stopped his counselor in the middle of the session and said, "I understand what you're saying, and I understand the definition of focusing, and I understand what visualization means, *but I can't throw strikes.*"

The sports psychologist shrugged and said, "Oh, you'll have to ask somebody else about that because I don't know anything about pitching."

It is not necessary to be a pitcher in order to work with pitchers on focusing. What is necessary is an understanding of competition and the mechanics of what the pitcher is trying to accomplish. Then this knowledge is factored into the equation so that the focusing support isn't merely a generic program pulled off the shelf. It's an individualized program. It's not enough to have people on your team who are going to help you focus and do the other things necessary to succeed. You have to understand where you are and where you need to go, then what you need to do to get there.

NEGATIVE AND POSITIVE MENTAL FILES

Each of us has two files in our central nervous system. Everything we do is stored in these files. One is a file that's overloaded and runs over. It is the file of things you want to avoid. These are mistakes you've made, things you've stored that you'd rather not do again. The other file seems to be relatively empty many times. It is the file that contains the things we want to accomplish. It is important to fill up and pull from the positive file instead of accessing the negative one, where you try to fight yourself and fight negative thoughts and fight the urge to avoid failure. It is a better use of energy to pull up something positive and execute to that.

Do you find yourself giving too much thought and energy to negative things? Do you fight these thoughts, asking: "Why am I thinking these negative thoughts? Why am I seeing failure? Why am I seeing myself not doing well?" You can look at this two ways. First, you can fight, fight, fight, and hope the negatives go away. But I have found a more productive way to handle negative thoughts is to *let them run their course.* This approach has proved to be very effective, regardless of the environment or venue. Let negative thoughts run their course, which doesn't take long. It may seem a long time but normally takes seconds. Once the negative thoughts have run their course — then replace them with positive thoughts.

For example, the negative thought may be: "The last time I met with this prospect, I didn't do very well." Okay. So you didn't do very well. But don't follow that by thinking, "Why am I thinking this?" Just let the thought run its course. Now immediately replace it with what you want to do. "I'm not running *away from* not doing well. I'm *going to* being successful. So what am I going to do in the next meeting? What am I going to accomplish the next time?" Determine what that will be and play it over and over in your mind. That prepares you for the next time, the next opportunity.

For example, if you're playing golf and you hit a bad drive, when you get ready for the next shot, your first thought is, "I hope I don't hit another bad shot." That's human nature. You may fight the thought and say, "How stupid I am to be thinking about this. It's crazy. I'm going to ruin my game." Instead, after you think, "I hope I don't hit another bad shot," let the thought go. As soon as that thought has crossed your mind, replace it with what you want to accomplish. You don't want to hit a bad shot. What do you want to do? You want to hit a good one. So you don't want to make a bad presentation. What do you want to do? So you don't want to be a bad parent. What do you want to accomplish? And so forth. Again, you have to know what you are *recovering to* in order to move ahead, to succeed, to win. And you need to know what level of performance you want to reach.

You must let your support system help you. Many times you will need other people around you to talk with you about adversity or simply to listen. Most of us have the information and the vehicles needed for recovery, but we need the support system for positive reinforcement that helps us move to the next level of achievement.

To sum it up, *when a negative thought pops in your head, let the thought run its course,* which takes a matter of seconds. Then immediately replace that negative thought with something you want to accomplish. And remember, when you have recovered from the adversity, reward yourself. Go to dinner.

Do something as a reward for your achievement, your winning. This is important. It must not be overlooked. It's a waste of time and energy to fight the negative thoughts. What you do instead is gradually replace those negative things with positive things. And that enables you to focus easier and faster.

The rule in focusing is: It is extremely difficult to succeed if your focus is directed toward avoiding mistakes. You need a plan to help you focus better, so that it becomes fun and a part of what you do every single day. For that to happen, you need to know what influences focus.

FOCUSING STARTS WITH SELECTIVE ATTENTION

In order to focus on anything, you have to have something in your system that tells you the correct things to focus on. In other words, you need to have the correct experiences, also called *entry behaviors*, when you come to focus on a situation. Otherwise, you end up focusing on things that you can't execute or don't need to execute. You need selective focus, knowing what exactly the cues are. Information processing is the starting point.

How do you receive information? Once you receive information, what happens to it? There is a basic process of receiving, packaging and decision-making that takes place in the central nervous system. To make a very complicated issue very simple, you receive information through four or five different mechanisms. You experience it, you touch it, you hear it, you see it. The information is fed into the system and is processed, then packaged. There is a mechanism in our system that functions like a colander. It sifts out the negative, bad or useless information. We package the good stuff. It's put into a package that we call "perception." That package then is sent to the decision-making level of your nervous system. A decision is made on what the appropriate action might be, then the proper muscles are activated and you execute. That, in a nutshell, is what happens.

In order for those things to happen correctly on a regular, consistent basis, you must be able to focus, which involves "selective attention." If you try to teach a four- or five-year-old child how to catch a ball, you will see that they fatigue early when they start the training. That is because they do not have selective attention. Instead, they key on everything in the universe. They see you. They see your arm. They see the ball. They see birds flying in the background. They see the trees and the leaves blowing. They see cars driving in the background. They see people running. And then there are psychological noises. They hear and see everything that's going on. In the middle of that whole process, maybe they'll catch the ball.

Once they learn how to catch the ball, everything begins to change. They understand that there are only a few cues they need to follow to catch the ball — such as your arm motion and the ball. In other words, they get very selective in their attention. Then it makes no difference what's going on around them, what's going on in the background. They lock in, they focus, and therefore they don't use as much mental energy. They don't fatigue as fast, and they can play a lot longer.

LEARNING "THE HARD WAY" IS GOOD

Too many times people get into environments, both professionally and personally, where they are asked to focus, but the peripheral factors around them are so great that they cannot exercise the selective attention process essential to focusing well. It ends up being a trial-and-error effort.

A few years ago I did some research in error-free and trial-and-error learning. Two groups were equal in abilities, but they took different approaches to learning a motor skills task that involved moving a probe through a maze. Every mistake was electronically recorded. When the error-free group started in the wrong direction, the monitoring system stopped them before they committed the error and redirected them. The trial-and-error group made mistakes, but kept trying until they made the correct decisions. The task was completed when each participant completed the maze three consecutive times without error.

Then after a few weeks we brought both groups back in to do the same tasks. The results were surprising. The trial-and-error group had very few, if any, errors on the retest. The error-free learning group, on the other hand, had almost as many mistakes as the trial-and-error group in the first test.

Conclusion: In many cases when you're trying to lock in and focus on something, it's not an unhealthy process to work your way through and *find out which cues are appropriate and which ones are not.* You learn what calls for a response and what to discard as opposed to having someone tell you. Your retention is better when you go through the trial-and-error learning process. It may take a little longer to learn, but the retention will be significantly better.

Selective attention when it is negative can have a devastating effect. That was the difficulty for a college placekicker with whom I worked. When he came to me, he was very frustrated because his attention was not on his kicking, but on an old leg injury. Every time he would start to kick, he would wonder if the injury was going to get worse, if he was going to be able to kick. It was an injury that had bothered him on and off for several years. Before he tried to kick, he would even catch himself tensing the muscles in that leg just to see if the injury was still there. Obviously, his focus was on trying to not hurt himself as opposed to trying to be successful as a kicker.

The remedy involved the kicker's going through a visualization process in which he could mentally see himself executing the kick correctly. Then when the ball was snapped and the holder put the ball on the ground, the kicker would repeat to himself a trigger that took him to the ball: "Be aggressive, good contact, good leg swing." This enabled him to pull together everything he'd seen mentally together so he could focus and lock in on kicking the ball.

The result: He became a great kicker and in the process was injured much less than he'd been before. It seemed like magic, but it wasn't. It was simply that he learned to supplement his talent by learning to focus on exactly what he wanted to do.

WHEN TO RELAX: "TIMED MENTAL LAPSE"

There is more to focusing than knowing when to focus and on what to focus. You must also know when to relax, when to give your mind a break so that you don't try to hold focus too long. It only takes a few seconds to take a mental break. If you use this process it will eliminate mental fatigue late in any situation, and you'll eliminate most of your mental errors.

Those athletes who say that they go into the zone and stay there for three or four hours may not realize it but they're not going into the zone and staying for three or four hours. Emotionally, your system won't let you do that. Your system is going to take a mental lapse whether you want it to or not. And it is definitely more beneficial to choose to take a break *between* executions, whatever your work or task.

Inconsistent emotional levels often involve a mental lapse. This is a problem commonly and openly discussed in sports. But it's never acknowledged in business, because in that venue it's embarrassing. People constantly experience mental lapses in meetings. Everyone has. You're in a meeting, trying to pay attention, and there's an imaginary tap on your shoulder. It's your system telling you, "Stay and listen if you wish, but I'm going outside for a walk." That is a mental lapse. Your consciousness, to a large degree, leaves a shell of a person sitting there. When it returns, you don't really know how long it's been gone. It is a frustrating situation. Or you drive the same route every day and don't pay attention to appropriate cues, or signs, and suddenly you miss an exit or a building. You were doing all the mechanical things correctly, but emotionally what happened was very close to self-hypnosis.

The most common definition of a mental lapse is "loss of concentration." It can range from a fraction of a second to minutes. That's enough time to pose a major detriment to performance. A mental lapse was blamed for a base-running error that cost the Atlanta Braves the 1991 World Series, in the view of many people. I don't agree that one play like that should make the difference, but it is true that a mental lapse occurred in a high-pressure situation.

When control is lost momentarily, the blame lies with an internal short-circuit. Think of the times when you were talking with someone and suddenly you lost your train of thought or lost attention momentarily, completely missing what was said. During a conversation, you need to check two things periodically: 1) Are you paying attention? 2) Is the other person paying attention?

Here is the major difference between winners and survivors: *Winners have timed mental lapses.* They do have the dreaded lapses, but they control the occurrence and the duration of the mental lapse. They concede that their emotional system needs a break. But they maintain close control over even the lapse. It is not a random event. It is controlled by the winner.

The most destructive impact of a mental lapse occurs when no decision is made during those critical seconds. Look at it from the perspective of its effect on total performance, and you'll recognize that just a few seconds or milliseconds have made the difference in victory and defeat. In fact, many times no decision is worse than a wrong decision, which at least gives you somewhere to start.

Learn to regulate the mental lapse, and the positive results will be significant. This involves learning how and when to use selective relaxation. Learn that during a timed mental lapse you are able to promote better and higher emotional control. You eliminate the loss of energy caused by needless recovery from a lapse. You control when you are going to have it and when you are not.

Your mental system's ability to package information will improve when given a break. If, for example, you practice too long or sit in a meeting too long, then you experience diminishing returns. In other words, the longer you work, the worse you get. After a short period of this "overwork," also known as "overlearning," take a long break of several hours, come back to the work or practice environment, and you will actually start performing at a higher level than when you stopped the previous session. The "downtime" gives your system an opportunity to gather and package the learned fragmented information so that correct decisions are more easily made.

KEY 6

See It Correctly —
Do It: Mental Practice

How important is it to practice mentally? If you are physically talented or you have the knowledge to execute on the
job or if you think your parenting skills or your mechanical
skills as an athlete are good, then why should you engage in
mental practice?

The answer is compelling: match two people with equal
physical talents in a competitive encounter, and the person
who performs stronger mentally will win most of the time. In
working with some of the best performers in the world for
the last 25 years, I have found that the winners are not necessarily more talented than their competitors, but they are
much better prepared mentally. They are better organized.
They are able to visualize. They are able to recover quicker.

Mental practice is an extremely valuable tool. It is used
for two primary purposes. First, it enables you to review your

competencies, to motivate you and to give you a picture to guide you in executing, and that's the way it is commonly used. Mental practice is also useful as a learning tool. With this tool, you actually can learn a skill or you can learn sales techniques or many other things. Basically, if you can see what you want to do in your mind, then you can execute it mentally, practicing until you "package" the skill.

It seems incredible, but some people can learn to play sports before they ever try to do so physically. I know two individuals who have done this. One of them learned to play golf, at the basic level, before he ever picked up a golf club or teed up a golf ball. He did it by watching videotapes and then visualizing himself executing the drives, the putts and the other shots on the golf course. The other person became a fairly proficient tennis player simply by mental practice, visualizing himself playing the game. Using the techniques of mental practice, he learned the basic skills that enabled him to become a reasonably good tennis player in a very short time frame. Once he started to play, his proficiency accelerated remarkably because he had the basic skills firmly in his mind.

There is much more to mental practice than simply seeing yourself execute skills the right way. This chapter will show you how to practice mentally, what to practice mentally and what to avoid. Once we've looked at the mechanics of the whole process, then you will be equipped to take whatever you do and plug that activity into this basic model for mental practice, and it will make you better professionally and personally. There is no question about that because it will make you more comfortable. It will reduce your anxiety level before you start to execute. It will enable you to lower your post-performance anxiety level quicker.

Research shows conclusively that mental practice is effective in performance enhancement. My colleagues and I, as early as the late '60s and early '70s, conducted research with free-throw shooting in basketball. We had four groups of basketball players who participated in the study. They were: 1) a control group, 2) a mental practice group, 3) a physical practice group, and 4) a mental and physical practice group.

All four groups were equal when they started. Each group shot 25 free throws to start the seven-day study. The control group did no practice. The mental practice group stood on the free throw line every day for seven days and mentally practiced 25 free throws and walked away. The physical practice group came and shot 25 and walked away. The mental-physical practice group mentally practiced 12 or 13 free throws and then finished up physically with 12 or so free throws every day.

When the groups came back to be retested a week later, the no-practice group, predictably, had the worst results. The mental practice group scored significantly better than the no-practice group, indicating that, at least at a basic level, skills were learned without actual physical participation. If you think it through, do it correctly and have all the parts in place you actually learn the skill. The physical practice group, as expected, performed better than the mental practice group. Next, the mental and physical practice group went to the line. This group performed better than the other three groups. Similar results will be found for almost any motor skill that's been researched over the years. It a true indication of the value of mental practice.

MENTAL PRACTICE: EXECUTE CORRECTLY

In the last chapter, we talked about how people receive and process information. If you receive and process information correctly, keep only the proper cues and then put that package together and store it, that gives you the entry behaviors necessary to practice mentally whatever you have stored. However, if you stored mistakes and you mentally practiced mistakes, then you will execute mistakes.

This process very often fails because of flaws in the mechanics of mental practice. One of those mechanics is speed of practice. It is critical that you mentally practice at actual speed of whatever you intend to do. Obviously, if you mentally practice at a faster speed, you set yourself up to execute physically in fast motion. If you visualize in slow motion, then you actually set your body up to respond in slow motion. It is a prerequisite to know how long it takes to execute a given skill so that you can mentally practice that skill in real time.

In baseball, it's possible to tell if the pitcher is using true visualization. It's simple. I ask him to step back, visualize the pitch, step up and throw; then he steps back off the mound, takes a quick breath, steps up and throws and says, "I saw it." He claims to have visualized the correct pitch. My reply: "You must have seen it faster than I could see it because you only took one second to do it." If in fact he did see it in one second, he set himself up to fail simply because he is going to overthrow, or he is going to speed up his motion, and it's not going to be natural. So it is imperative that you visualize in real time.

VISUALIZATION — BE REALISTIC, BE POSITIVE

One of the most significant impacts of mental practice is an attitudinal change. Positive anticipation of an event at least provides an opportunity for success. People can foresee and be prepared for the consequences of their actions if they have worked through the visualization process and anticipated the consequences of their actions. This is another critical factor in performance.

It is absolutely essential that you know what your capabilities are. You need to know what talents you have. You must understand what your entry behaviors are, and you need to visualize those. But be careful in your visualizing not to go overboard. It is not only frustrating but also discouraging to visualize things that you are not capable of executing. You always need to stretch your system and visualize things that are going to stretch your abilities. But you should visualize realistic skills that you are capable of executing, given your talents, your tools and your mechanics. What you visualize is something you may not have done before but are capable of doing, reaching a higher level of performance within your capabilities. It's common sense.

A pitcher who is able to step back from the mound, take a deep breath, visualize the next pitch — which takes about three seconds — then step up and throw that pitch, has more confidence and motivation. Visualization becomes an incentive to perform better, and many times the results will be consistent with the visualization.

If you make a speech, then review it later and visualize a bad opening or punch line, then the next time you try to avoid the mistake, the probability is high that you will repeat the mistake. You want to avoid the incorrect visualization because it causes, or at least sets you up for, incorrect performance. Only look to previous experiences to make mental corrections. *Avoid 20/20 hindsight.* If you are involved with the corporate environment, you only look to previous experiences to make corrections and move ahead. You don't dwell on negative experiences or previous experiences that had negative aspects. If it's over, it's over. You go to the next action. Never go into the execution of what you want to do by performing off the previous execution. In other words, don't perform off mistakes.

Hitters visualize a swing. Hitters step out of the batter's box, and they visualize themselves swinging and hitting the ball. They step back in and they try to execute to that visualization. Golfers are the same way. If a golfer wants to avoid carrying baggage when he hits a bad shot, he steps back, visualizes a good shot and then steps up and executes according to what he replayed in his mind. Even without a videotape for reviewing and aiding visualization later, if a golfer hits a great shot, steps back and visualizes, or replays, that shot he is storing positive information mentally for future use.

If you have a great sales meeting, then before you leave the meeting or immediately after you leave, you need to find time to be alone and visualize what just took place in the meeting. In this way, you can store that data and execute the same way again. Don't visualize and think about the things that went wrong. Visualize and execute mentally the things that were correct. You will build a good mental data package for drawing on at the next meeting.

Parents can visualize conversations they are going to

have with teachers or with their children. Or conversations they are going to have with each other. By doing this they are able to anticipate questions that might come up, anticipate conflicts and the consequences of actions, which can be very effective. Teachers should use visualization as a daily process before classes. The execution of any activity will benefit from the visualization process.

YOU MUST "SEE IT IN COLOR"

One of the top international tennis coaches, Dennis Van Der Meer, once defined true visualization at a tennis clinic. "True visualization is when you can see it in color," he said. A pro golfer recently made the same comment. The idea is that in true visualization, you can see everything. You can see your clothes. You can see the course. You can see everything that's going on around you, and that gives you a vivid picture of what you want to do and how you want to do it.

The whole visualization process means that you mentally see performance from beginning to end. You don't just see the end result.

If you visualize the sales meeting and you only visualize signing the deal, you have no mental preparation or mental storage of what got you to the point where the deal was signed. A golfer would have no mental storage of what caused the ball to go where he or she wanted it to go.

True visualization is seeing everything from start to finish — and don't ever leave out anything. With the whole sequence in mind, you can make corrections in your performance, or make adjustments in how you are communicating with people.

In visualization you get to the point where if you want to make a change in whatever it is that you are executing, you can plug in the change you want to make and then continue to visualize. You can make changes in performance through visualization before you ever execute. That is a benefit of visualizing very specific, correct things.

To visualize correctly, you may need to describe the activity and create a specific list of segmented events making up the "total package." The example below, using golf as the subject, shows you the sequence in this process.

EXAMPLE

Before trying to visualize, break down the parts of your swing, starting with club selection and ending with follow-through. Then place that shot breakdown into the total sequence outlined below:

1. Select club

2. Visualize:

    a) Address

    b) Take-away

    c) Backswing

    d) Swing

e) Contact

f) Follow-through

g) See ball flight

3. Physically address ball

4. Use "trigger"

5. Execute shot

6. Mentally store good shots

VIDEOTAPE: AN EFFECTIVE TOOL

Visualization is most effective if you can have yourself videotaped — everyone needs a videotape of his or her performance if possible. As an aid to my own speaking, I have videotapes of past speeches and seminars. When I work with golfers, I videotape every swing — including drives, long irons, short irons, sand shots, approach shots, fringe shots, putts. My objective is to provide each golfer with a videotape of what that golfer is able to execute. I do it with every sport. I do it with football — with linebackers, with quarterbacks, with defensive players. Videotapes are used extensively with baseball players, with pitchers, with hitters, with guys who have problems with throwing.

The videotape gives you a ready-made picture that you can pull up at any time. If possible, get a videotape of your performance and run it a number of times. It is not uncommon for me to repeat a certain pitch by a pitcher 10 to 15 times back-to-back on a videotape so I can bombard his system with what he is able to execute. Then it's easier for him to mentally pull out that picture and execute. This holds true in other situations.

Salespeople consistently improve their presentations by videotaping them and then playing them back, per the process described. Consequently, they use less time visualizing, and consequently, expend less energy. They are also more successful more often. Use of videotape, where possible, can be a critical factor in visualization.

THE MECHANICS OF VISUALIZATION

CRITICAL ELEMENTS IN VISUALIZING:

In visualizing as a mechanical process, these are the critical elements:

1. Always see yourself executing correctly.

2. Always mentally see correct techniques.

3. See everything involved in every part from start to finish. Repeat: *every part from start to finish.* "See it in color!"

4. Visualize the action *at actual speed.* If you omit parts or you can't visualize clearly certain parts, then go back and start over. Don't ever muddle your way through and store incorrect material.

5. Remember you are trying to develop total confidence and mental consistency. That's your goal in visualization.

6. Repeat the mental practice several times during each session. Do not mentally practice one time and execute. Mentally practice several times, and don't rush. This deliberate visualization will enable you to set yourself up so that you are motivated and you have an incentive to execute. At that point, you almost get anxious to execute.

7. When you reach the place where you are going to execute your skills, visualize everything just before performance.

Once the mental process becomes conditioned, you won't necessarily have to do it every time, but you need to pick your times to do it. If you need to make changes in whatever you are performing, then you only need to pull the mental picture into the conscious mind and plug in the execution and do it again, and again. Repeat the initial process until the change is a part of the conditioned response when you are making corrections.

Remember that the prerequisite to the success of mental practice is that you must know how to execute correctly and know that you can do it. This means that: 1) you don't *think* you can do it; you don't *wonder* if you can do it: you *know* you can do it; and 2) you visualize only correct skills. This is critical. If you mentally practice mistakes, you are going to make mistakes.

Any time you feel you are losing concentration or you are losing your rhythm or losing focus, then you use the visualization process. You can key in your concentration by simply verbalizing to yourself a key word or phrase — a trigger (remember the placekicker who told himself, "Be aggressive, good contact, good leg swing"). If you visualize a conversation, and then you walk in and you are ready to start the conversation you might say something to yourself such as, "Go for it," or something that is significant to you. Choose a word or phrase that pulls everything you visualized back to the front of your mind so you are able to execute. The trigger is critical to performance. It actually brings your mental practice to physical realization.

KEY 7

Speed of Recovery:
A Critical Skill

YOU NEED THIS SKILL EVERY DAY.

The word "recovery" usually conjures up thoughts of overcoming an extremely negative condition or circumstance. Usually when we talk about recovery, people assume it involves terrible problems, even tragedy. That is not necessarily the case. Everyone is confronted daily with situations from which they need to recover in order to return to a desirable level of performance. In business, people constantly recover from conflict, crisis and stressors. Salespeople daily have to recover from rejection. Several times a day, at least, a parent must recover from the frustrations of rearing children and carrying out the normal routines of running a household. Athletes have to recover from setbacks and lapses. Hitters must recover from slumps. Pitchers have to recover from bad pitches. There is the need to recover daily in every walk of life.

It is critical that you learn to recover from adversity and to do so quickly. This ability separates talented people who win consistently from talented people who win occasionally, lose or just survive. If you know the technique and you have a process in your mental files that enables you to speed up your recovery from adversity, then you are going to perform better for a longer period of time than people who don't have the recovery technique or process. Quick recovery from adversity is a critical skill, personally and professionally.

Nearly everyone with talent will win on occasion. Sometimes people are described as winning by accident, and that happens. Given the right circumstances, you can win if you just show up. But on a daily basis, that is not the case. Talent alone does not ensure winning, though it is a prerequisite. But you also have to be totally committed to what you are doing and what you want to achieve. Granted, part of the equation for success is being in the right place at the right time and getting the right breaks. But this kind of good fortune alone will not guarantee success without the other parts of the equation. Long term, you must have the capability to recover from misfortune or adversity.

SPEED OF RECOVERY:
A LITTLE ADVERSITY NEVER HURT

In my judgment, the speed of recovery ranks among the most important variables for success, yet it is seldom discussed in "success" books. If you have talent then you recover in time — but the key is learning to cut down on the time interval. There are two ways to do this: 1) When you're beginning to experience adversity, if you understand what's happening, then you can counter it; 2) when you hit bottom, you can learn to recover back to the level where you were previously. Even though you always play to win, it's healthy to lose sometimes so that you learn to recover. Granted it is not what you want to do. But it has to be a part of life. You will find losing an almost insurmountable barrier to performance if you are so talented that you have never felt the need to learn mental skills for fast recovery. Unfortunately, in the case of some athletes whom I have known, people refuse to even concede that adversity could ever rear its ugly head in their lives. That attitude makes adversity a very difficult problem indeed.

A friend who was an outstanding high school football coach compiled an enviable record of 54 consecutive victories, which won him a place in the Coaches Hall of Fame. His players never lost a game from the eighth grade until they graduated from high school. Many of the youngsters then signed major college scholarships.

But something unexpected happened. After a year or two, many of those players showed up back in their hometown. They had quit their teams. They had quit not because they lacked talents or intelligence but because they had begun to lose games, to make mistakes or not perform as well as they had. And their ability to recover was minimal. The reason was that they had never experienced adversity, and therefore they had never learned to recover from it.

Take the case of a college pitcher who was signed by a pro team. In his senior year of college, he had a record of 15 wins and 0 losses, making him a top draft choice. When he arrived in spring training, he discovered everyone on the team was just as good as he was, so that even when he was pitching well, he wasn't winning all the time. The result? Terrible anxiety problems that forced him to quit the team after less than one year. But it was not due to any lack of talent. It stemmed from his inability to recover from adversity. He had never learned how to recover when he made a bad pitch or lost a game. Again, recovery is critical to sustaining performance, to winning.

The same principle applies to employees who still have their jobs after a company has gone through reengineering and cutbacks. In such situations, more efforts should be made to teach the employees to recover quickly from adversity. This, too, is critical for the company. These employees will be required to do more work, to increase their productivity and in some cases to give up the proper balance in their lives because of greater demands on them — creating additional adversity from which they need to recover. They also face another challenge: They no longer have as strong a support system as they had with fellow workers who have departed the company. The luxury of a relatively deliberate recovery is gone. Quick recovery is required.

ADVERSITY IS REAL: DARK TUNNELS AND OTHER PITFALLS

How do you learn to recover quickly?

The first step in this process is to accept that adversity is real. It is a daily experience in life in most environments. Next, assume that you will be better by having gone through the adversity recovery process. Understand that you will learn from the experience. You will learn that you are a stronger person than you thought. You will learn that you can deal with conflict. You will learn that adversity is not going to stand in the way of pursuing your goals.

If you are to recover quickly, you must avoid the dark tunnels. Dark tunnels are filled with your past mistakes. One of the worst habits of many people is that they spend most of their time looking at mistakes they've made and replaying them over and over, concentrating on avoiding those mistakes. It is good to review your mistakes if you then develop a plan based on pursuing a goal or goals that will make you better. Otherwise, dwelling on mistakes is like drinking poison every day. The result of this approach is that many people who encounter adversity never recover to a successful level, to winning. Instead, they recover to surviving and, unfortunately, they begin to feel good about where they are.

Think about how long it takes you to recover from adverse situations. How long do you carry the baggage around? If you are in sales and you make a presentation at 9:00 in the morning and get kicked out at 9:05, how long is it before you're back to being yourself again? Is it three hours? Four hours? During the time it took you to recover, how many people did you turn off? How many did you upset? How many sales calls did you miss? How many potential closings? If you are honest with yourself, you will find that adversity cost you significantly, not only in terms of financial reward but also personally in terms of your relationships with other people. If as an executive or a supervisor, you make a controversial, difficult decision, how long do you replay it before you move ahead — as opposed to making the decision and moving ahead immediately?

Winners recover quickly. Winners recover between pitches, not between hitters. Winning hitters recover between swings of the bat, not between times at bat. Winning salespeople recover between sales calls, not between days. Winning tennis players recover between shots, not between points.

And recovering quickly is difficult, without question. The mechanics may be easy, but recovery is difficult to sustain, to keep the commitment. When adversity comes, you have to want to recover. You must make a daily commitment to play to win every day.

UNDERSTAND THE RECOVERY PROCESS

Certain things are necessary in order to understand the recovery process.

FIRST, YOU HAVE TO DEFINE WINNING.

This enables you to know when you have recovered back to winning. For a golfer with whom I worked, poor putting had become his adversity, and, in this case, winning meant standing over the ball confidently, seeing the line from the ball to the cup, and stroking the putt with certainty. It was a matter of loss of emotional control, and we worked on how he could recover it. Finally, he reached the point when if he prepared to putt and didn't have a confident feeling, he stepped back, took a deep breath and visualized a good putt he had made. That restored the appropriate emotional level, and he putted better than he had in months.

SECOND, YOU MUST LEARN TO RECOGNIZE THE SIGNS OF ADVERSITY.

It does not always hit you in the face. There are subtle signs: You begin to feel uncomfortable in the task or performance. You become anxious during performance (whether work or sport). You feel too much tension. You become unsure of yourself. You become tentative about your presentation. When one or more of these symptoms appear, you need to start the recovery process.

A typical reaction to adversity is to ignore it and attempt to move on. However, this can result in a worst-case scenario that requires much more time to recover than if you act quickly when you encounter difficulties, mistakes and failure. Consider another example from golfing. Some players whom I counseled had failed to make several tournaments or performed poorly when they made the cut — and then called for assistance. If they had called after missing the first cut or after the first three bad holes, then their recovery would have been accomplished within hours. Instead, it took weeks to effect their recovery. Players who want to correct things in their game after years of doing them the wrong way expect to fix the problem in one or two days. Recovery doesn't work that way. Think of it as analogous to any addiction. The longer you smoke cigarettes, for example, the longer it will take you to break free of the craving and recover to being a nonsmoker.

THIRD, YOU MUST LEARN TO VISUALIZE.

You have to see yourself mentally managing adversity and succeeding. As covered in the previous chapter, Key 6, it is essential that you store successful performances in your mental files. These positive entry behaviors must be on file for use when needed. On occasion, you should mentally recall an adversity and then follow it with visualization exercises of how you successfully managed the adversity. The most important variable is experience. You can develop a pattern of recovery through visualization relatively easily. Visualization facilitates your learning to focus during adversity. Focusing enables you to develop a plan to pursue success and to recover.

FOURTH, SELECTIVE ATTENTION IS A PREREQUISITE TO RECOVERY.

Keep your eye on the ball, to use the well-worn expression. For sports involving balls, this is a critical issue of selective attention. A golfer who hits into the sand must focus very selectively to get out of the sand. This used to cause me terrible anxiety on the golf course. "I'll never get out of the sand," I thought. Then a teacher told me, "If you focus on hitting an inch to two inches behind the ball, you'll get out of the sand." It worked, and now the sand traps don't raise my anxiety level. If there is something that automatically causes adversity for you, then you need to confront it head-on and develop actions to deal with it. The next time it comes up, you will be able to recover.

FIFTH, YOU MUST REALIZE THAT WINNERS ARE EITHER VERY POPULAR OR VERY UNPOPULAR IN THEIR ENVIRONMENTS, NEIGHBORHOODS OR HOMETOWNS.

Other people may be jealous or resentful. Survivors may be more popular than the winners — because the winners set a standard that the survivors do not appreciate or accept.

You may find that you are bucking the system when you try to win. That happened to a fifth grader who was very bright. He set a pace that was uncomfortable for his classmates. They began to intimidate the youngster, make fun of him and ridicule him every day. The student soon became frustrated and confused. His grades fell, and then his tormentors left him alone. He was no longer a threat. But three years later in a different school where intelligence is respected by his peers, the youth has a positive attitude and his grades have improved. The recovery has been a long, slow process, and if he had been removed from the negative environment sooner, his recovery would have been much quicker.

SIXTH, YOU MUST UNDERSTAND HOW YOUR WINNING AFFECTS OTHER PEOPLE DURING THE RECOVERY PROCESS.

Other people must become involved in helping you recover to the point that you are again a contributing member of a team. This is not only in sports but also in the corporate environment and in the home as well.

SEVENTH, THE RECOVERY PROCESS REQUIRES PATIENCE.

Obviously, this is true of our physical health, yet some athletes as well as other people are so impatient and aggressive by nature that they try to shorten the natural healing time, the recovery time. You need to be patient. Sometimes you will find this the most difficult part of learning and practicing recovery.

Parents in particular must understand that children don't change overnight. Sometimes it is one step forward and two steps backward before the pattern is reversed and becomes two steps forward and one backward. In the corporate environment as well, patience must be shown in helping people to recover or change behaviors. This is a valuable tool for employee retention. In sports, post-injury patience is a worthy challenge. The rule of thumb is simply patience and persistence.

THE MECHANICS OF RECOVERY

How you view the process is all-important. You are not recovering *from* something. You are recovering *to* good performance. Never run *away* from things. Always go *to* something.

When something negative happens, back off mentally — then see yourself performing the skill or task or engaging in an activity correctly. If it is a conversation that didn't go well, immediately afterward take a few minutes to yourself and replay the conversation. Don't wait. Determine what went well and what could have been done better. *Determine how it will be better the next time.* Then the next time you are performing the skill or engaging in a conversation there will be little, if any, adversity because you have made the corrections beforehand.

If you don't have a videotape available to provide you the replay to recover in your mind, then when you perform the skill or task or engage in an activity and do it well, then take a few minutes and replay that success. If it was your best performance — whether a speech or a sales call, a decision or a sports skill — then immediately afterward take a few seconds and replay it so that you store that correct performance in your mental files to be called up when needed. Every time you do this, you are storing behaviors that you will recall to recover when necessary.

In your free time, visualize your past successes. This exercise, repeated over and over, will enable you to achieve faster recovery from the negative impact of adversity. Think about how adversity tastes. It tastes bad. It looks bad. It feels bad. And you do not want that taste or look or feel of the bad, negative effects of adversity. Now you know the quickest relief is what you have stored mentally, and you use it to work on recovery. Use the worksheet that follows to remind yourself of the steps that can help you to recover from adversity, both personally and professionally.

RECOVER FROM ADVERSITY

1. Review your assets and liabilities from Key 1.

2. Analyze the present situation (the adversity).

3. Review the goals you are trying to achieve.

4. Determine which assets can be used to offset this adversity and achieve the desired result.

5. Write down specific actions which will lead you to success.

6. Prioritize these actions and begin to recover.

KEY 8

Win with Emotion

FIND THE "MENTAL EDGE"

Coaches often talk of playing with emotion and the importance of "the mental edge." What do these expressions mean? Can a performer be too emotional? Given a high level of talent, emotion probably does separate the winners from the survivors. Emotion can raise talent to an even higher level, not only for individuals but also for teams — sports teams, corporate teams and family teams.

Uncontrolled emotion, however, can be devastating to performance. Too many times we see the downside of emotion rather than the upside. This leads to encouraging people to relax instead of encouraging them to be emotional. But my philosophy is that, with the exception of the "timed mental lapse" discussed in Key 5, *if you want to win, you never relax during performance.* It makes no difference what the performance might be, whether it involves sales, sports, business or family — do it with emotion. Perform at as high an emotional level as you can control.

In crisis and conflict, uncontrolled emotions are a serious liability, while controlled emotions can provide a tremendous asset to finding solutions. Emotion is consciously used in recovery from adversity, in focusing techniques and concentration. Great players push their emotions to the highest level they can control during performance. Again, this is true both in the sports environment and elsewhere.

Getting to the emotional edge is a vital part of this program. The question that has to be answered is: What is your emotional edge? On a scale of one to 10, what's the optimal level of emotion for top performance?

If you're a one, not emotional at all, you're too relaxed. Lacking emotion, you are not tuned in to what you need to do. Your performance is very low. You tend to make errors of omission. You don't have the selective attention discussed in Key 7 dealing with mental practice. Without selective attention, you will merely respond to cues at random, some relating to performance and some not relating.

On the other hand, if you are up around the 10 level, too emotional, then you tend to make errors of commission. You react to every mental cue you get. Recall the selective attention example of a small child learning to catch a ball and responding to every cue that's visually possible — cars, trees and other things in the background — until the catching skill is developed. Then the child recognizes the important cues and locks in on the person throwing the ball, on the arm, the release of the ball and the flight of the ball.

Given the ideal situation, the optimal emotional level will be six or seven. At that point, you are on the emotional edge, at your highest level of performance.

GETTING TO THE OPTIMAL LEVEL

How do you get to that level? How do you sustain that level? And if you go over the edge, how do you get back? Not how do you relax, but how do you get back to the edge? And since the emotional edge is so important, why not start the day at six or seven and hold that high level of emotion throughout the day?

First, if you reach that level in the morning and try to hold it all day, your nervous system won't allow it. It just will not permit you to hold a high degree of concentration for a very long time. Everyone's system needs a break, a mental lapse. The key is to control your system and control when you take a mental break, as described in Key 5, as opposed to letting your system take a break on its own.

Second, most people don't raise their emotional level to six or seven for a simple reason. They are afraid. As a society, we're afraid. We are afraid to play or perform on the emotional edge consistently because of what might happen. If you make a commitment to perform at the edge, then you have conceded that at some point you will go over the edge. Obviously, the closer you are to the edge, the more stimuli you will react to emotionally and the greater the chances you will go over the edge. For example, if you're in thick traffic in the morning rush and you're already on the edge, when some driver cuts in front of you and stops, then you're more likely to go over the edge. If you're in the same traffic but at a three or four emotionally, and the same thing happens, then your irritation may send your emotional level to six or seven but you'll still be under control.

There is a time to reach the edge. And I am convinced from experience that if you are not willing to go to the edge and take some risks emotionally, then you're probably never going to win consistently. You may win on occasion because of your talents alone. But you won't be able to use your emotions as a supplement, one of the keys that separate winners from survivors.

CONTROLLING YOUR EMOTIONAL EDGE

Just what does it mean when you go over the edge? It means you have become so intense, so high that you are out of control emotionally. You are not then making conscious decisions. Your emotions take over. No one wants to be perceived as out of control. You appear to be a dangerous person. You have that "look."

You will be less fearful of going over the edge if you know that you can retreat from that emotional level and if you know how to do so. If you know that in your mental files you have what's needed to regain control, then you will be more willing to play or perform on the edge, which is essential to winning at the highest level. If you don't have what's needed to regain control, then you are likely to stay relatively far from the edge, and, therefore, far away from winning at the highest level.

How do you get back if you go over the edge? Many people in the corporate environment, on the job, in the office, experience tension mentally in the afternoon. It drives people away from having conversations, from meetings, from making conscious — and often critical — decisions. These people are over the edge emotionally and realize they will not make good decisions. What they need is to let their mental "tape" rewind.

If you are over the edge, take 10 minutes and let your mental tape rewind. You do this by diversion. Close the door. Listen to music. Go outside and walk around. Lie down and take a 10-minute "power nap." You should find a quiet place and get very comfortable, while giving yourself the suggestion that you are going to lie quietly for 10 minutes. It may take several times for this to happen, but eventually, your system will become conditioned, and you will be able to drop off to sleep and wake up 10 minutes later very, very sharp. You will have the energy you need for the rest of the day. This is one way to bring yourself back from the edge.

Find a diversion from the work routine. As a parent, you can take a ride or go shopping for a little while. Divert your mind to break the cycle.

Progressive relaxation also will bring you back. If you're going over the edge with frustration and tension in your neck and shoulders or arms or a headache, you can learn through practice to isolate different muscle groups and perform exercises to relax the tension. Eight to 10 minutes of these exercises will restore your equilibrium.

Don't fear playing or performing on the edge emotionally. It's a wonderful place. It's the best place to be. The problem arises when you don't take a break. Instead, you may become more frustrated and then go further over the edge.

Athletes graphically illustrate this point: Some athletes who have had a losing experience on the field will go into the locker room, sit down and read a book — and regain control. Some athletes who are very religious will go into the locker room after a bad outing and read certain scriptures — and regain control. But there are other athletes who, after a bad performance, will turn over tables, kick lockers, take baseball bats and attack the plumbing, or throw water coolers on the playing field, throw towels, gloves, helmets and bats — you name it. I've seen basketball players and coaches throw folding chairs on the court. A football player on the sidelines got so frustrated and so far over the edge that he ran onto the field and tackled the ball carrier. I've seen out-of-control coaches punch players. I've seen CEOs so frustrated and out of control that they go into the office and wreck it, verbally and physically, ruining a relatively good environment.

GOING TOO FAR: BURNOUT

If people don't create a way to regain emotional control, burnout is inevitable. Take the situation when a person's job is not going well, driving the emotional level higher and higher. How many people call home and say, "I'll be late for dinner," because they feel they need to add hours to the day? If they usually work 10 hours, they add three hours. If they usually work five days a week, they start working six days a week. They add hours rather than analyzing the 10 hours of work and trying to get more out of that time. Instead, by routinely adding two to three hours, they are setting themselves up to spend most of the added time emotionally and not productively. Then how many of those people after a while don't even call home anymore because it's assumed they'll be late for dinner?

The backlash comes on the personal side of life with more tension and emotion resulting from not being home for dinner. When you add two or three hours to your working day and then make it part of your lifestyle, you have stolen that time. You've stolen it from your family. You've stolen it from your friends. You've stolen it from your leisure time. You've stolen that time from the very side of life that is the motive for your work in the first place.

That is why I keep asking the question: Why do you do what you do? If you never understand this, then taking time from your personal life is a nonissue. If you do understand why you do what you do — and still steal time from your personal life, then your frustrations eventually will drive you from your job. You will wake up one morning and hate your job because it stole your personal life.

If you keep working long hours and the mental tape keeps getting tighter and tighter, eventually you're going to wake up one morning and while you're in the shower, you'll hear a strange *flap, flap, flap*. It means your mental tape has self-destructed. And you can't replace it. When it's gone, it's gone. That's the worst-case scenario. You have to make a conscious effort to play with emotion every day but to keep it under control, consciously. Before you get caught up in your job or sport or anything else, stop and think about the ramifications and the toll that uncontrolled emotion takes on your life.

A WINNING EMOTIONAL EDGE

You have to understand and recognize the symptoms of going over the edge to know where that point is for you. Mentally record feelings during performance when you are successful. Do this immediately afterward, before you leave the environment. Mentally replay what you just did, and store that successful experience. When you store it, you not only input the mechanics but also the emotions of the experience. This enables you to know when you are reaching that emotional level again. Visualize this again and again and again. Repeat the process until the emotions are stored with the mechanics.

A few years ago I worked with a pro baseball player, a great hitter. But he was inconsistent. Sometimes he was great, and at other times he was terrible. He had fallen into a bad slump. He couldn't hit, and he was trying to not miss, to not make mistakes, to not look bad, as opposed to swinging to hit the ball, to be successful. We talked about his problem.

"Can you remember one time when you hit a ball and it was like music? When it was vintage you, it was perfect and everything was in place?" I asked him.

Suddenly, that big athlete came to the edge of his seat, and his eyes began to well with tears. "Yeah!" he said. "It was against Philadelphia. It was the seventh inning, and it was cold that night. We were behind 3-2. The count went to 3-and-1, and I hit a fastball. It was inside, and I hit it. And it didn't even feel like I hit it. But it went over the fence. And it was a great feeling. We won." And he kept on talking about that hit.

"How many times have you thought about that hit since then?" I asked.

He looked surprised. "You know, this is the first time."

The information had been stored mentally, and when the hitter recalled the performance, he replayed not only the mechanics but also the emotional feeling he had.

Within a couple of days, the hitter came out of his slump. He started hitting as he had before. It wasn't because he'd changed the mechanics of hitting. It was his ability to recall the winning emotional level that enabled him to repeat the performance.

You can do that in every walk of life. You always store the information. It's just a matter of finding it and pulling it up. Although it's not an easy task, the more often you retrieve the information, the easier it becomes. The rule is that before any performance or activity, if you visualize a previous similar experience, it will serve as an incentive or motivator and also raise your emotional level to the desired point. Then if you should go over the edge during the performance, all you need to do is take a deep breath, visualize and return to the optimal level. You can do that in a matter of seconds.

BEWARE THE YO-YO SYNDROME

Remember, you do not want to relax. You don't want to fall all the way down to one on the emotional scale and then, immediately before a performance, have to climb back up to five, six or seven on the scale. Most people, however, engage in yo-yo emotions. They spend most of the day going up and down. At the end of the day, they are emotionally fatigued.

Everyone has what is considered a normal daily activation level. Here's how it works: Their emotional arousal level goes up to a certain point when they get up in the morning, dress and head for work or other activity. The level varies from one person to another. But they work off that base all day. Then it's up and down. If you're at work, and an important telephone call comes in, suddenly you have to elevate the emotional level because it results in better, quicker decisions. After the call ends, the emotions drop back to the base level, and you relax. Then you have to attend a meeting, and your emotional level rises again. But it returns to base level afterward.

The result is mental and emotional fatigue, not because you went back to base level but because you had to raise the level to make important decisions. It makes sense to go to the edge and stay there, eliminating the need to spend so much time and emotional energy going up and down. Staying on the edge, of course, is not a static situation. You will fluctuate up and down a little, but you will be able to hold a relatively clear line on the emotional edge all day when you have mastered this technique.

Note: You must understand a very important effect of staying on the edge. You will be perceived as a threat to people who are relatively relaxed and never rise above a two or three on the emotional scale. This means you have to be totally committed to playing on the edge. You also need to feel good about being up there on the edge and winning. You will reach the point that you are able to go to the edge and stay as long as you wish. You are going to do things that other people cannot do and achieve things they dare not try. This does not always create admiration and respect; in fact, it often engenders envy and contempt.

ANXIETY CAN BE HAZARDOUS

The most commonly discussed emotion is anxiety. By definition, anxiety is a generalized feeling of fear or worry about things that might happen or of the possible consequences of events that might happen. Unlike stress, which will be discussed in the chapter that follows, anxiety is sometimes hard to get a handle on, even though we talk a lot about it.

If this emotion were defined in stages, the first stage would be "becoming nervous." The majority of people say their greatest fear is speaking in front of groups. If you've done this, you know you get a rush through your system. You get high anxiety. Your voice may change. You get muscle tension.

The second level of anxiety is tension. It may result from a lack of knowledge or worry over the consequences of your upcoming actions.

The third level is fear. It stems from a perceived threat and can drive your performance higher until it reaches a certain level. Then it can drive you out of performance. It's often referred to as being "psyched up" and sometimes "psyched out," having butterflies, choking. If you reach that level and do not take control of your emotions, then you reach the panic point. That is the most serious level of anxiety.

The best antidote is patience, which is very difficult to practice if you are in a panic. Unless you have a vehicle in place to control your emotions, then you can develop phobias that may drive you completely out of a particular environment.

In working with athletes, I encounter this question constantly: "Do you motivate athletes in sports psychology?" To the contrary, more time is spent trying to get athletes under control and lower their anxiety than in motivating them.

Most of them are already motivated to be where they are.

In sports, a lot of players are known as "practice players." They perform like great champions in practice but don't play very well during the game because of their anxiety level. This is related to the fear of failure. The fear has crossed the point where it was an incentive to performance, and it has become a detriment to performance. It is common for aggressive athletes to work on raising the anxiety level of their opponents to drive down their performance level. And it works many times.

Of course, it can have a reverse effect. Raising the anxiety level can actually improve performance. So players roll the dice when they employ that device in a contest. You have seen this kind of psychological competition often in sports. It is the manipulation of anxiety levels between fans and players, between colleagues, between salespeople, between parents and children or between siblings. Nothing physical happens but there is a play on the anxiety level. For instance, when a game-winning field goal is about to be attempted, the opposing team will call a timeout to let the kicker think about it, to let his anxiety level rise and maybe impede his execution. It's also common in sales presentations. Some people want to go first. Others want to go last. It depends on where they are psychologically and emotionally, and what they believe is most beneficial to them.

CHECK FOR THE TELLTALE SIGNS

Look for telltale signs from your mental files to alert you when you're not where you want to be emotionally or you're over the edge. One sign is less efficiency in your performance. Another is freezing in high-pressure situations. Other signs are forgetting assignments and losing touch. Physically, in baseball, for example, a player may lose the feel for the ball. Even proneness to injury may be a sign. Athletes who want to play but are afraid of failure will find a way to be injured just before they are to perform.

A minor-league pitcher with whom I worked had major-league talent. But every time he got a call to go up to the major-league team, he would get injured. This happened three times. First, he turned his ankle. The next time, he ran into a wall. Then he hurt his back. He had a good career as a minor-league survivor but never pitched in the majors. It was the result of fear of success, an emotional issue. He was afraid to win even though he wanted to be a great competitor. He feared that if he won, his accountability would increase. So would the expectations for him, and so would his responsibility. Surviving was more comfortable than truly winning at what he wanted to do.

Many people encounter fear of success or failure, the loss of emotional control or ignorance of their optimal level of emotions. These controllable shortcomings cause a constant rising and falling in performance. You can be at 10 emotionally today and down to one tomorrow, then back up to 10 the next day. That is frustrating. But as you learn to understand your emotional levels and gain control of them, you can not only empower yourself but also help others to grow stronger and better, especially those closest to you.

It takes time and effort — sufficient practice time, playing time — to build confidence. It is very difficult to build self-confidence and self-concept if you never get to play or perform. The key is to motivate people to their optimal level, not too low and not too high. Maintain a consistent, sustainable emphasis on performance. Set realistic goals, but make them tough to stretch your system. Make them specific, but attainable, which is critical, and set time frames for your goals.

Anxiety is good when under control. You want your preperformance anxiety to be relatively high to get ready. You want it to slide back a little during performance when your anxiety level will increase as a natural consequence of your actions. Your post-performance anxiety may rise or stay even.

A vital part of dealing with anxiety and emotion is your team — your personal team or corporate team, sports team or other team. Here are practical exercises:

1. Have your team practice some situations that artificially create pressure.

2. Use verbal and nonverbal positive reinforcement to build confidence and self-concept.

KEY 9

Thrive on Stress

STRESS IS A FACTOR IN EVERYTHING

Stress is unquestionably a determining factor in winning versus only surviving. Stress is a factor in everything you do, both personally and professionally, every day. Winners thrive on stress. They are what I call "stress seekers." Survivors, on the other hand, expend enormous amounts of energy avoiding stressors. Consequently, they only survive, at best.

This will be surprising to you if you have always been told that stress is an entirely and even overwhelmingly negative influence in your life. How much time do you spend each day trying to rid your life of stress, and how much does stress cost industry every year? Billions of dollars are spent by corporations in dealing with stress, and much of that cost is in disability payments. Employees can retire from some positions with as much as 75 percent disability because of stress.

However, while it would seem that stress is a significant negative factor in terms of productivity and health, probably *more than 80 percent of stress factors are neither positive nor negative when they confront your system.* Stressors become negative because of perceptions. We hear the word "stress," and we start thinking of all the things that are wrong with our lives. We very seldom think of the positive things that act as incentives to make us become better. Stress management seminars are very popular as a way of teaching people how to eliminate stress and how to relax. But too often these seminars are nothing more than knee-jerk reactions to a traditional definition of stress. The truth is that your mindset causes most stressors to become negative.

By definition, stress is the amount of wear and tear on the body. Stress has a physiological impact — for instance, stressors are with you when you walk, with stress on the joints in your legs. When you throw, there is stress on your arms and shoulders. When you talk, there is stress on your vocal cords. When you breathe, there is stress on your respiratory system — and sometimes these physical stressors develop into psychological issues. So there are stressors everywhere. There is also the "psychological noise" in the environment that can cause stress or distress — things like the crowd noise in sports, horns blowing in traffic, and even colors of clothing, wall colors and the pictures in offices are all considered psychological noise.

The list below shows stressors taken from actual lists compiled by 1) a professional businessperson, 2) a professional athlete and 3) an individual who reported on personal stressors. These are typical, not atypical. These common stressors, if dealt with, give you an opportunity to make your life better. The key is to recognize which stressors you can control and which ones will control you if given the chance.

STRESSORS

PROFESSIONAL	PERSONAL
1. Deadlines	1. Marriage
2. Quotas	2. Lack of personal time
3. Budget	3. Children
4. Coworkers	4. Lack of exercise
5. No communications	5. Travel
6. Vague expectations	6. Finances
7. Uncertainty	7. Expectations
8. Customers	8. Society indifference
9. Being able to deliver	
10. Finances	
11. Travel	

STRESSORS MAKE YOU WHAT YOU ARE

Stressors make you what you are and drive you to be where you are. They can drive you to the emotional edge, get you where you need to be in emotional arousal in order to attain an optimal level of performance. If they don't drive you to become better, stressors may make you worse through illness, depression and burnout. Stressors can drive you to fail. The outcome depends on your perceptions. The operative term is "perception."

Because of conditioning, both personally and professionally, people tend to panic when under great stress. They let stress take control of their lives. This happens often with young people. It is not an issue just for only the older or middle age person. This is an issue for everyone. I've known parents whose five-year-old kindergartners were in counseling for stress in their environment. I've known people no older than 26 who have had heart attacks related to stress. Stress really does not discriminate. It affects everyone.

In the workplace, stress-related problems cause such widespread symptoms as headaches, nervous tension, irritability, complaints of burnout, wasted time and very poor time management. All contribute in some respects to absenteeism, which is a major issue for businesses.

To repeat, up to 80 percent of stress is neither positive nor negative. Traffic is an obvious example of something that stresses, yet isn't inherently negative. Others are deadlines, financial resources or lack of resources. People are stressors. Children are stressors. Bills are stressors. Almost everything you can imagine that affects your life creates some degree of stress. All these stressors can become assets to your productivity or they can become detriments. Every day we have stressors that will be put into either the incentive/positive shelf or the detriment/negative shelf. Choose to put those stressors, if at all possible, on the positive side of life.

The key is how you deal with stress, and that is a conscious choice you make.

At one point in my life, I was partially paralyzed. The diagnosis was a stress-related condition for which I had to be hospitalized (though I have never been sure if that was the problem or if the diagnosis of stress was simply convenient). Nevertheless, when I recovered, I began to do ten times as much I did before. My productivity soared. I took better care of myself. I exercised more. I had better nutrition. I looked at things from a different perspective. Since then, I've never been happier personally or professionally.

The impact of stress can be devastating. There's no question about it. But the impact can also be rewarding if we choose the positive approach.

TYPICAL STRESS REACTIONS

Think about some typical stress reactions that you have probably experienced:

(A) "I'VE GOT TO GET OUT OF HERE."

This reaction means you are trying to run away from stress. At times the right response is to withdraw from stressful situations. If you're involved in conflict that is stressful, it may be a time to get away and engage in strategic planning. It may be a matter of minutes or hours before you come back and confront the stressors. But don't think for a second that if you withdraw, the stressors will go away. Most of the time they don't. The decision to let time take care of it is usually the wrong decision. If you choose to withdraw from stress, do it strategically — with a purpose and plan for coming back and facing the stress.

(B) "I CAN'T DO ANYTHING ABOUT IT."

I think everybody has experienced this reaction. Everybody has felt it. You feel you have no control at times. Some people experience it in traffic every day, going to and from work. Situations come up where you try to state your position and meet with a lack of interest or a negative reaction or no reaction at all — then you feel out of control and that you don't have any impact. This is especially common in the corporate environment, where it can seem as if you don't have any impact on change. That's a very helpless feeling, and it generates more stress.

(C) "TAKE A DEEP BREATH AND KEEP IT INSIDE."

This is potentially the most dangerous of all reactions. I don't think that stress actually causes heart attacks and strokes, but stress certainly sets your system up to be more vulnerable because it weakens the system's defenses against heart attacks and strokes and other diseases.

If you are prone to holding things inside, exercise provides a good outlet — providing the exercise itself is not a source of stress! For example, a person may decide to end a stressful day with a game of tennis or some other competitive sport. I played tennis with a CEO one afternoon. It was obvious to me that every time he served and swung his racquet to hit the tennis ball, in his mind he was slapping some colleague across the head with it. He was more frustrated when the match ended than when it started.

Exercise on a regular noncompetitive basis is probably the best route to take. That way, you have an outlet, you don't keep the stress inside, and you don't get the ulcers, the rashes and other problems. Swimming, running, jogging, walking or walking on a treadmill can all be low-stress activities. It's often helpful to attach your exercise to something else you feel is important for you to do. For example, my best time to exercise is during the 6 o'clock news, when I can have an hour of exercise while I listen to the news. The exercise doesn't take away from anything that I want to do and does not cause stress as a result.

(D) "I WANT TO TAKE CONTROL OF THE PEOPLE WHO CAUSED THE STRESS."

The stress becomes a control issue. This is far too prevalent among corporate managers and creates havoc when the team should be pulled together as opposed to being pushed apart. It happens when someone feels uncomfortable because of stress and tries to control everyone else in the environment. This is not a positive way to manage yourself and your own emotions. Control can get to be very comfortable if people submit and let you control them. You can be a pretty good survivor using that technique, yet nobody around you gets any better because everyone's under your control. You don't get any better. At best, you will always be a survivor.

(E) "I THINK I'M GOING TO SCREAM!"

A good scream might be healthy sometimes. I think it's something everybody's done, and it's probably not a bad idea in the right place and at the right time. But remember that a sudden emotional outburst of 30 seconds may cost you years of loyalty and respect from members of your team — your personal team and your professional team — and may require 30 days of rebuilding the relationships wrecked by the explosion. People who are quick to have emotional outbursts feel better afterward — and assume everybody else feels better. Wrong. If they were objects of the outburst, they would quickly see how inappropriate it is as a stress management technique! This is, at bottom, just passing the stress along to someone else.

(F) "BRING ON THE STRESSORS. THEY MAKE ME BETTER."

This is the best reaction. It is the key to using stress positively. Again, stress will either kill you or make you great. The choice is yours. The best way to start is to take time to identify all your stressors, both personally and professionally, and decide which stressors can be easily changed to assets. For example, if you have stressor "A" now a liability, what can you do to make it an asset? What can you do to change stressors so that they become incentives as opposed to detriments to performance? The answer: *Write an action for changing each stressor.* These actions must be difficult but attainable and each must have a time frame attached so that you can evaluate whether or not you are dealing with stress in a more productive way.

Even so, there will remain a small number of stressors that are probably just always going to be headaches. They are always going to be there. They are a part of your life or your job or your family. If you cannot turn them into incentives, they may be potential detriments to performance. When those negative stressors emerge, you need to use the visualization techniques learned earlier and visualize what you want to accomplish — not the stressors you want to avoid. Eventually they become much less of a problem and may have only a negligible effect on your life.

Part of this visualization includes verbalizing to yourself that you are better after having dealt with a stressor. A golfer with whom I worked had a substantial lead in a tournament, but it slipped away and he lost. This created a lot of stress for the golfer. He had to step back and look at his situation and try to pull the positive things out of it. He had to tell himself: "I was in a position to win. I went through conflict and had to deal with it. There were a lot of positive things that happened. I hit some great shots. I made some key birdies. The other person happened to make more birdies and won. That's a negative thing but that's part of the sport, part of being a risk taker, of playing to win. That's part of learning to thrive on stress because, given that situation again, I will probably have a different, more productive reaction."

When you select stressors that you want to change and use as incentives to performance, first choose those that will give you a feeling of accomplishment and fulfillment almost immediately. As you move those stressors to the positive side of the ledger, take on the tougher stressors that may be longer term in payout but will make a significant difference. You are accomplishing things along the way to make the tougher stressors incentives to performance.

KEYS TO HANDLING STRESS

When stress attacks the central system and goes to whatever part of the body is affected, the body becomes alerted that something is out of order. After considering all the evidence available, the system makes a decision to react to the stressors. The decision may be to eliminate the stressor, to tolerate it or to simply ignore it (probably the least desirable and possibly the most destructive to your system). The best solution is to deal with stress successfully by conditioning the system for the stressor or by eliminating the stressor. In most cases, there is absolutely no good reason for letting stress cause physical or mental problems in our system.

There are many things you can do to deal with stress, both for yourself and the people on your team. The following are keys to handling stress:

I. TIME MANAGEMENT:

Learn how to take more control over your time, to control the things you can control. That can be a critical step in eliminating time-related stress. If you survey people in the work environment today, where most companies are trying to get more productivity from fewer people, you will find that time management is a major issue. People don't "have time" to do so and so. My position is that everybody has time. We can always find time to do things we want to do.

II. COMMUNICATION:

This is a very valuable stress management tool. It is something that happens every second of every day. But to reiterate, communication is not technology. It is not faxes. It's not e-mail. Communication is talking with people. You communicate even when you avoid communications. You say something when you walk away. You say something in your expressions. You say something in almost everything you do. Physically, you say something. There is a cliché: "What you are talks so loud that people can't hear what you say."

Many stressors would be managed positively if communications were positive. This is certainly as much a personal issue as a corporate issue, including communications with your spouse, your friends and your children. It also involves teaching children how to communicate with each other. That will help them to learn to thrive on stress.

Efficiency is critical, but effectiveness of communication may make the difference in a person dealing with the stress of learning something new or succumbing to stress and withdrawing from the environment.

III. EXPECTATIONS:

Know what you expect of yourself and others. Let other people know what you expect of them. This is a major step toward reducing stress in the environment. A large percentage of people leave jobs every day, not because they don't like the job or the environment or the pay. They leave because they are never told what is expected, specifically, of them. They are told to work hard and do their job, which says nothing. Without specific expectations, frustration and doubt and confusion may cause a very stressful situation, leading to the "fight or flight" syndrome. For many people, the natural reaction is just to leave and go somewhere else.

IV. EXERCISE:

Wholesome exercise need not be competitive, but it should stretch your system. A program of regular exercise as simple and easy as walking daily or three times a week can do wonders for physical and mental health, including relieving stress.

IV. BALANCE IS ALSO A MAJOR STRESS MANAGEMENT TOOL:

For everything that's significant professionally, you need something personal that's significant. You must have balance in your life. It helps remove not only personal stress but it also helps to remove workplace stress.

V. KEEP IT FUN:

People need to learn that they can have fun while being productive. Attitude is a major issue. We need to strive to create an environment where all employees can enjoy their work. They don't have to laugh and hug or dance on the job, but they can receive fulfillment and enjoy being productive. Sadly, there are some places where it's very difficult to find anybody smiling at work. Nobody wants to be in those environments. Some people get locked in and are miserable until they retire. Create an environment that people can enjoy.

To summarize, you will feel better by learning to handle stress. It is a part of your daily life and always will be. Stress doesn't have to be negative unless you perceive it as negative. If you did not have budgets and deadlines and other stressors, then you wouldn't be very good at what you do. We all need deadlines and timelines to be productive.

Stress is a wonderful thing. Remember this thought. Repeat it over and over: "Stress is a wonderful thing!"

MAKE STRESS WORK FOR YOU

A. LIST YOUR TOP 10 STRESSORS:

1.   6.

2.   7.

3.   8.

4.   9.

5.   10.

B. FROM "A," LIST WHICH STRESSORS CAN AND SHOULD BE AIDS TO YOUR PRODUCTIVITY:

1.

2.

3.

4.

5.

C. INDICATE THE ACTION NECESSARY TO CONVERT EACH STRESSOR IN "B" TO AN ASSET:

1.

2.

3.

4.

5.

D. FROM THE "A" LIST OF REMAINING STRESSORS, CHOOSE THOSE WHICH CAN AND SHOULD BE ELIMINATED:

1.

2.

3.

4.

5.

**E. INDICATE THE ACTION NECESSARY TO
ELIMINATE EACH STRESSOR IN "D."**

1. Make your actions specific, difficult
   and attainable.

2. Attach a time frame to each action.

3. Evaluate the actions and use them to
   make stress work for you!

KEY 10

Environment:
Critical Performance Factor

THE MOST NEGLECTED INFLUENCE

The physical environment, whether in sports or business or home settings, is probably the most neglected influence on performance. It's also one of the most critical determinants of performance outcome. How many times have poorly performing athletes been traded to different teams only to become high-level performers? Several cases of this "worst-to-first" scenario have occurred every year in professional baseball over the past 10 to 15 years. Athletes struggling with a poor batting average have gone to another team and raised their batting average 30 to 40 points. There may be some influence from the different manager, coaches and stadium, but probably the determining factor is the change in environment.

Look at almost any new sports stadium, and you find a tremendous difference in the environment provided for the home team as opposed to the environment provided for the visiting team. It ranges from the colors of the walls to the size of the space to the amenities — all environmental factors. The same holds true in the business environment, in schools and even in the home. It is most evident in the school environment. When you go into different schools, it is revealing how cold some classrooms are and how warm others are.

The environment is fascinating because it is there every day — not only the physical environment, but its psychological components and the people who are a part of the environment. A lot of money and time are spent motivating people — only to send them back into a negative environment. How do you create a motivating environment? How do you enhance the environment in such a way that motivated people want to be there?

READING THE ENVIRONMENT

How do you read the environment? How do you walk in and determine if there is a positive, motivated environment or a negative environment or a neutral environment? How do you evaluate the physical properties of the environment? Psychology students are taught to look at the furniture, the wall colors, the pictures and other things when they go into an office. They learn to read the environment and learn something about the person from the physical environment. What is "psychological noise"? How does it relate to the environment? There are various ways that noise can play a role. For example, baseball fans in the early '90s made much of the physical environment at the Minneapolis Metrodome with regard to the outcome of the World Series between the

Minnesota Twins and the Atlanta Braves in 1991. The environmental factors at play there were: 1) the noise, 2) the white hankies that every person in every seat was waving the whole time, 3) the white ceiling that made it hard for fielders to see fly balls, and 4) the very closed-in nature of the stadium. The environment obviously constituted a tremendous home-field advantage for Minnesota, but it posed a serious disadvantage to the visiting team. All the distractions might well have influenced the outcome of that Series which the Twins won.

Restaurants may use fast music to turn tables faster if they depend on a high table-turn. A high-ticket restaurant with a low table-turn ratio may play slower music so people can sit and relax. Bars that depend on a high percentage of alcohol sales will play faster music, which means people tend to drink faster. Piano bars, where selling a lot of alcohol is not a priority, will play slower music. These are forms of psychological noise.

Other examples are evident in most sporting events that we attend. Camera flashes can cause distraction. In fact, one click of a camera can throw a golfer's swing so out of sync that it will cause bad shots and even bad tournaments. If you have watched a World Series game — or, in recent years, Mark McGwire of the St. Louis Cardinals or Sammy Sosa of the Chicago Cubs at bat — you know that with every pitch and every swing of the bat, there were camera flashes all over the stadium. Unless players are conditioned and the disruption becomes almost a part of the environment, cameras and flashes constitute psychological noise in the environment.

POSITIVE ENVIRONMENT = RECORD PRODUCTIVITY

One of my corporate clients makes over 300 million pounds of French fries a year. They asked me to work with their employees at a plant located in a small town in a desert area of a northwestern state. Once a month I visited the plant and worked with the people there, trying to create teamwork and to develop management.

I wanted to get a feel for what they did, so I went into the place and worked two 12-hour shifts back to back. It told me what I wanted to know about the environment. It was not stimulating. It was depressing. It was extremely monotonous. Over a year's time, making monthly evaluations, I saw no real change, and I learned that the employees had become so conditioned to the environment that it did not rate as a concern to them. When new people came in, they did not perform very well and were not very productive. But the people who lived in the town, most of whom worked in the plant, were conditioned to it. From the outside, I saw a deadening environment. But the perception from the inside was: "It's a job. It's a way to make a living." It obviously was what they needed to do to survive.

The executives of the company did not live in the town, but rather in large cities considerable distances away. Clearly, they were not tuned in to the culture of their plant. They didn't understand the issues, and therefore, felt no need to make changes so long as production held at an acceptable level. Yet production could have been maintained and, at the same time, the employees could have enjoyed their work and had more fulfilling personal lives if the company had embraced changes that were proposed in my program.

I had suggested they start recognizing performance in the workforce. Awards such as time off, or dinner certificates (to the one restaurant in the town) or cool gifts — winner's choice. I also wanted to put a jogging track around the plant, along with some recreational equipment to be used during break time. In addition, I felt that someone on the workforce should be on the management council. None of this was magic, of course, just a sign that ownership cared about the people. But those changes were never made.

If you're going to influence the environment in the workplace, then you need to do something more than a short motivational session in a once-a-month visit as those executives did. You need to be a part of the environment so you can feel it, you can touch it, you can understand what people go through on a daily basis. Only then are you prepared to make productive changes.

Not too long ago, corporations went through a phase of having employees take "ownership" of their respective jobs. The term became overworked and went the way of "quality" and "excellence" and other buzzwords. I was called in for guidance at such a company, one that had asked its employees to take ownership in a plant environment that was not clean, lacked areas for the employees to take a break and finally, had no restrooms. The workers used portable restrooms similar to those seen on construction sites. You can imagine the effects of this environmental factor.

When I met the administrators, I suggested that we try something different. I said, "Instead of trying to motivate the employees and pushing them to take ownership in something that I certainly would not take ownership in, why not try to change the environment and create something they enjoy being around?"

So we brought in mobile homes and converted them into break areas furnished with showers and changing rooms for the employees. Then we made an effort to find out what the employees enjoyed doing. Among their favorite pastimes were hunting and fishing on the weekends. The company then leased several hundred acres of land and invited the employees to hunt and fish on the property. The company put a track around the plant so that people could walk or jog during downtimes. Basketball goals were erected and horseshoe pits laid out near the plant.

In other words, the company created an environment where people could take a short break, change clothes and enjoy recreational activities, relieve their stress, then shower and change before returning to work refreshed and invigorated with a positive attitude, a winning outlook.

As a result of these changes over a four- to six-week period, the employees achieved new production levels within the next three months and afterward maintained those record levels. The company never changed the people, never changed the equipment and never changed the techniques of how they operated. But the company changed the environment. So the employees felt some excitement. They enjoyed going to work. That company's experience clearly illustrates the impact of environmental factors.

People are not likely to buy into something that is not appealing to them. I think the most valuable investment that a company or a team or a parent can make is to provide an attractive environment so the key players want to be there. Again, a tremendous amount of money is spent on motivation and motivational speakers when that money could be spent more effectively in creating a positive environment. It is self-defeating to motivate people and send them back into a negative environment. Motivational sessions may be effective over the short term but if you are looking long-term, the environmental issues will probably shape the productivity curve in most endeavors, personal or professional.

ENVIRONMENT — COLD OR WARM?

Parents, how many times have you gone into a classroom and thought, "I would have a hard time learning in this classroom"? It was not warm. It was not inviting. It was not motivating. You knew that your children did not enjoy being in that environment. However, it is very difficult to change such a situation, and you may have to change schools because of the negative classroom environment.

Take the school environment that is very cold and non-family oriented, that resents family members visiting with their children at school or having lunch with them. Compare that to another school that invites family participation. The school administrators love to have family involvement. They prefer a social atmosphere for the learning process. The teachers are involved with the students and welcome input and feedback from parents. Doesn't that sound like a much healthier environment for children? It's an incentive to learn. It's the kind of place that may make you wonder, "Where was this kind of place when I was in school?"

At least some companies in the business world are learning this lesson. I know a sports marketing company that owes much of its success to a minor but extremely important practice: When an employee is not performing well, the owner of the business does everything possible to put that person in an environment where he or she can succeed. Instead of just firing the employee, in whom the company has already made an investment, the owner first tries to solve the problem by modifying that worker's environment. It makes good business sense — and it's also humane.

Enjoying your work and seeking to please customers rank as the top priorities when creating or modifying the environment for positive results. This fact struck me when I worked with another restaurant company. Again, as a way of preparing for the challenge, I worked in the restaurant for a week, trying to get a feel for how people felt about their jobs. It was fascinating. I worked in the kitchen, where I discovered that those employees were very proud of what they did. And, surprisingly, they became very protective of their specific jobs. If I tried to help them do something, at first I was rejected because the employees took a great deal of pride in what they did. It was their job. They wanted it done right, and they didn't want to give it up or any part of it. Several days went by before any of them let me do anything other than sweep the floor. That business proved to be very successful because the management promoted an environment that encouraged people to enjoy their work, which showed — and, as a result, the customers enjoyed their dining experience and wanted to return again and again.

People tend to neglect so many things that are environmentally related. Everyone should spend some time thinking how he or she would have done things differently with respect to the environment, given another choice. It's amazing that so many people look around their environment but don't seem to notice what's important. Consequently, they don't learn anything. When you are in an environment, whether it's at home or school or in a business or sports setting, you should be able to look around you and learn how to manipulate the environment, if necessary, in order to facilitate the enterprise and move to the next level.

LEARNING FROM OUR CHILDREN

When did you last go to a playground and watch children play? They create games and make up rules. Then they play the game. They reach an outcome and they go home. Remember when you were eight to 10 years old and some of the creative things you did? Most of these were facilitated or even were determined by the environment. Perhaps there was a lack of resources or equipment or other things that caused you to be creative in the environment. The things you did may have been off-the-wall in a grownup's world. But now you see them as creative.

A favorite question of mine at every convention is: "How many of you here today are as creative as you were when you were children?"

No hands are raised. Yet the truth is that everyone is as creative today as they were as children. It's just that when we become adults the size of the box gets smaller, we get more reserved, and we don't want to say creative things because people around us might think that we are "strange." Stop and think how many millions of dollars have been made on such goofy, childlike ideas as Hula-Hoops and Beanie Babies and Pet Rocks. Yet people as a general rule tend to grow more and more content, to live inside that small box and survive on the traditional way of doing things.

In fact, we surround ourselves with things in the environment, whether it's personally or professionally, that basically curtail our creativity: things that make it so easy that all we have to do is push a button to get things done. We don't have to do creative things to be successful, so we stifle any ideas we might have that would make us more visible, make us more accountable and make us obviously a lot better at what we do.

It seems to me that creativity is nothing more than unused common sense. It's just sitting in there waiting to jump out. Commonsense things that kids do, for example, are often very creative — ways to negotiate better, how to settle arguments or how to deal with conflict, how to engage in wholesome competition, how to play to win, even how to recover from adversity. If you have ever seen two children get in a fight on a playground, unless an adult gets involved and messes up the whole deal, the kids get over it and they go eat a sandwich. It's a done deal. They recover. But if adults get involved, then it's prolonged for days and sometimes weeks.

The creativity and positive impact of children on the environment struck me on a trip with the family to the Gulf Coast of Florida one year. Because the beach house had been relocated by a storm board by board, when it was rebuilt we had to do a lot of painting. So I was upstairs painting when my six-year-old daughter came into the room and announced to me that we were going to play school. "You're my student and your name is Lloyd," she told me. I said fine and went on with my painting, she left the room and I thought that was that. Well, a couple of minutes go by, the door flies open, she runs in the room, and says, "Okay Lloyd, I've had enough of your lip! I am going to call your mama. You're in time-out."

There I was, 54 years old and sitting in a corner painting a little spot because I'm in time out and I don't want to get in any more trouble. If you are a parent, you know what it's like to find yourself a part of your children's environmental creativity. And it is great fun. So we need to facilitate that more in children, but an even greater need is to facilitate this creativity in adults, in the corporate environment and in the world around us.

THE ELDERLY — ANOTHER GREAT RESOURCE

Another neglected learning resource, at the other end of the spectrum, is the old folks. And I am not necessarily talking about seniors. I am talking about old folks. Why do we neglect old folks? They are a critical part of our environment. And I don't know why when people get to be 60 and 65, corporations seem to think that they can kick them out without changing the environment for the worse. It's not that businesses don't need young blood and young energy coming into the corporate environment. They do. But we have an invaluable resource in the older people who have experience, not in technology or related skills, necessarily, but in the corporate culture. Their knowledge and experience are fundamental components of the corporate environment. And, obviously, the longer they've been around, the more they have to contribute along these lines.

I recently attended a convention for a large retail industry where I asked the audience this question: "Wouldn't it be fun to have a panel of former retail people who had spent their whole careers in the retail industry? We could put people who were 85 to 90 years old on the panel and ask them questions about how they sold their products and how they did different things in the environment without the technology we have." As I told these retailers, I think it would be a tremendous learning experience for young people. We just can't keep putting people out to pasture. I confess to total ignorance regarding age discrimination. To the contrary, I have learned most of life's important lessons from older people.

Look at the Atlanta Braves baseball team — since 1991, they have always had one person in their bullpen out of five or six who is a seasoned veteran. Even if this person never pitches an inning, he's worth what he gets paid because of his influence on young pitchers. He makes a valuable contribution by talking to young pitchers about how to recover from adversity, how to deal with different situations, how to pitch in cold weather, how to warm up — all things you have to have been at for 15 to 20 years to know. They are tremendous assets to the team and an essential and stabilizing part of the Braves' winning environment.

My grandfather is a good example of how an elderly person can contribute to the environment — broadly defined as the space in which we live and learn. I learned more from him about why I do what I do than I learned in 22 years of school. He was a welder on the railroad for 45 years, where he fixed the nicks on the rails. You are probably wondering what would motivate a person to do this for 45 years, what it was that took him from the nick on the rail to the next nick on the rail. The answer is dignity in work and pride in doing a job well. And because my grandfather constituted an essential part of my environment as I grew up, he communicated those important values to me.

I'm not sure you can teach that in seminars. I'm not sure you can learn it in school. I think it's there inside. You do something that's fulfilling and understand truly why you do what you do. Then you begin to have a level of pride in not only what you do, but maybe more importantly in who you are. These are the sorts of lessons you absorb from a healthy environment. They don't need to be in the books you read. They are in the air you breathe.

If you know somebody 100 years old or 90 or 95 you need to sit and talk with those people. I would guarantee you that afterwards you will know something you didn't know before; you might even begin to know why you do what you do. We need to rethink the role that our older folks play in creating and maintaining the environment around us.

KEY 11

Finding Your Balance —
and Keeping It

BALANCE IS A DAILY ISSUE

Balance is more than just a physical parameter impacting performance. Winners interpret balance to mean much more than physical equilibrium. Balance is a concept that has become a major issue in the lives of most people. It's a topic at many conventions, especially in meetings where spouses are involved. The major issue is that of achieving balance between the personal and professional sides of life.

There are very specific issues of balance within your personal life. If you are a parent, how do you balance time with your spouse and your children? How do you balance time between the children? How do you find personal time for yourself?

If you are a management professional, how do you balance your job within the corporate environment? Do you push some employees too hard while neglecting other employees? What if you have one person who is not motivated and five people who are self-motivated — do you spend a lot of time motivating the one person, or should you be more concerned with the performance of the five good people?

It is critical that a manager understand balance in order to deal with employees successfully. Many companies have committed a fatal error, which is to think that everyone can be motivated and that what motivates one person will motivate another. You must understand that every day of your life, balance is a challenge.

How many people today work longer hours than in past years? As evidenced by the number of corporate reengineering announcements and the cutbacks in workforces, companies expect more productivity from fewer people. That usually means more time away from home for the employees. Most people in high-productivity environments work longer hours than they did in the past. It's not necessarily a negative development. You should work long hours when you absolutely have to do so — but do not make long hours a permanent part of your lifestyle.

Achieving balance seems to be an impossible task for many professional people, and for many parents as well. Spend some time around moms and dads who have three to four children, and you realize it is incredibly difficult for them to keep balance within the home. They may feel as if they never have any time to themselves, as a couple or individually.

Even children now must be concerned with balance. How many obligations do children have these days? More than we had when I was growing up. When I was a youngster, we played a sport or two and went to school. Now there are so many extracurricular activities and in-school activities that children have a hard time maintaining balance in their lives.

Everywhere that I have included a "balance" component in my program, it has generated more comments than any other single segment of the presentation. People are hungry for balance, and they are asking for help. This is a dramatic change from just a few years ago. And as a result, I've come to believe that we as a society are beginning to understand the importance of balance in our lives. We are beginning to understand about fulfillment, about meeting our basic needs and helping those around us meet their basic needs. I think we are making progress.

IT'S QUALITY, NOT QUANTITY

If we look at quality of time as opposed to the number of hours, which I think is necessary, how many of us have lost our balance? I find that an alarming percentage of "successful people" in corporate positions, in the community, civic clubs, and the family are unhappy and unfulfilled because they have lost their balance and they don't really have any idea about how to correct the issue. They work longer and harder and then use the old excuse that they financially provide for their family and that's their job.

Winning requires balance. Coming in first demands intensive training and devotion to a daily routine. That takes commitment to work. Incredible amounts of time are required to achieve perfection in performance or even for the pursuit of perfection. Therefore, most of the time spent is skewed toward work. It doesn't mean you lack good balance. The quality of time spent is the critical issue. People who are devoted and who are good at what they do are usually going to work long hours. But again, the key to balance is the quality of time spent.

A challenging assignment for me was working with a group of promising young sales managers in management-development sessions. We met every month, first as a group, then individually. In the one-to-one meetings, the conversation often turned to the issue of professional versus personal interests.

"I have no time," was the complaint heard over and over. "I have no personal time and I don't have time for my children."

Balance was a major issue in the lives of these young professionals. As is so often the case these days, their goal was to work long and hard and retire at 35. Some of them worked seven days per week, sometimes 15 to 18 hours a day. No time for family, no time for friends, no time for themselves. Productivity, paradoxically, was less the focus than hours spent. A very simple philosophy prevailed: need more money, work longer hours.

We used the 12 keys to help them be more aware of where they were, where they wanted to go, whom they wanted to take with them, and, realistically, when they wanted to get there. We also set goals on the personal side of life. Then each person kept an hourly log for a week to determine how time was spent and what was accomplished. We were looking for common threads running across every day, similar tasks at similar times, and so forth. I was looking for time slots for self-reward as well as time slots for learning opportunities. For some in the group, I had to actually plug in "family time" until they began to understand the value of spending time at home. Sad but true.

The good news is that after three months of my work with those sales managers, every person in the group summarized the course with comments about balance: "I'm grateful for these meetings because I have balanced my life," wrote one individual. "I finally feel good about me and about what I do and about my role professionally and personally," another wrote.

I've seen major-league athletes with tremendous talents never make the grade and even be released by teams because they never learned to balance the peripheral things around the game with playing the game. When that happens, it may be too late to save a career, in sports or in business, or to salvage a personal relationship. I have worked with athletes who have played better after dealing with things peripheral to the game. When rookie players come to the major leagues, my first conversation with each of those players goes like this:

"You can *play* or you wouldn't be at this level. Now your major issue is to learn to *live* at the major-league level. In other words, learn to *balance your life*. Learn how to rest and get enough sleep. Learn when to do each of the things you have to do." It takes some athletes a couple of years to do that.

Start-up businesses in the Electronic Age are especially susceptible to being imbalanced. The lure of the prospective payoff on the back end is so great that people work a staggering number of hours up front. And they are rolling the dice, because the business may not succeed.

My question to the start-up workaholics is this: "What have you done to your life, and what have you done to your personal relationships, if there is no payoff?"

You should never put your entire life into your job. You must never give up the personal things in your life. Always retain quality of life on the personal side. Just because you're at home a number of hours does not mean that you have balance. You have to be there not only physically. You have to be there mentally. And it has to be quality time. It may be just staying at home. You don't have to plan a lot of activities, but you need to have that quality time in order to say that you truly have balance — if you want to have balance.

In speaking at conventions, when I emphasize the urgency of gaining balance and maintaining it, some people get very uncomfortable. From my observation, most of the ones who don't like the idea are at the executive level of their company.

At a team-building seminar for a major consulting firm, I talked with the senior partner of the firm before the seminar in order to evaluate the topics and the points to be covered.

"I saw your videotape," he told me. "And I loved your material. But I want to ask you to avoid talking about that balance issue with my people."

"Sure," I laughed, thinking he was kidding me.

The grim look on the guy's face told me he wasn't. "I don't want my people thinking that when they leave this meeting with you today," he said, "that they will be free to leave the office before 8 o'clock at night. I don't want them to think that for the sake of this balance you're talking about they don't have to come in on weekends, either."

It was sad. It was shocking. But that is how people are used many times. When I talked with his employees, many of whom were young, single, high-energy people right out of college, I had a very difficult time omitting the part about balance, which those people needed so badly. Even though I didn't talk about it as a topic, I slipped in some references to balance within other topics. I feel an obligation to do that whether or not I ever get invited for another seminar at that firm.

THE LONG AND SHORT OF IT

Adding hours to the day is not the answer. There isn't much evidence that if people work 13 hours versus 10 they will be more productive. The key is to explore ways to get the production needed within the time frame planned for the work. A corporate executive once told me, "I'm proud to say that I have spent 16 to 18 hours a day in this job my whole career." "Fine," I replied and left it at that. But I don't know that there is any job worth 18 hours a day of your life — or one that would even require close to 18 hours a day. It does not make sense to routinely add hours to the day.

If business is tough, your employer may call you in and say, "We need to get more done. We need to increase business." Immediately the tendency of some people is to add more hours to the day. If they're already working eight hours, they start working 11. If they're working five days a week, they add a day and work six. Then on the seventh day they are mentally still at work even though, physically, they're off.

These workaholics never stop to examine the 10- or 11-hour day. They never learn to find more productive time within a normal workday. Yet a great amount of research indicates there are only seven or eight hours of productivity within those 10 hours. I would suspect the same would hold true for productivity in 12 or 13 hours. It's like stretching four years of college into six. You stay busy and get the degree two years later.

Think about what is happening in your life.

If you are working a tremendous number of hours and you miss the things your children do growing up, do you not regret that over time? You may not hear that child say the first word or take the first step or catch the first ball or get the first hit or bring home the first A or get the first black eye or have the first emotional squabble or the first dance. Our kids don't do those first things twice. Of course, you can't possibly see everything your child does the first time, I am not suggesting that. But you should make an effort to do as much as you can with your children in terms of quality of time so that you don't miss *all* those things.

Think about it: You can't go back and talk about things you missed with your children once they are adults because they know you weren't there. So you need to make a commitment to attend to the important things in life, whether they involve your children, your spouse or someone else.

ACHIEVING BALANCE

Most of the time when balance is lost, it is gone before you realize it. Then retrieving your balance is extremely difficult. You get into a routine, get comfortable, and it's very difficult to change. Regaining balance becomes essentially a behavioral change, the toughest change for an adult.

Changing behavior with respect to balance may not always mean personal interests versus professional pursuits. The issue could be balance within the job itself. For example, professional golfers have a tendency to overpractice. They don't have much balance between the physical and mental practice. Hitters who are in a slump have a tendency to go to practice early every day and hit too many balls as opposed to balancing out the physical practice with the mental practice. If you're a hitter and you're in a slump, take a couple of days off. If you're a golfer and you hit three great shots in a row, then go on to the next club and practice with it. Hit three shots and then walk away.

How do you achieve better balance? The first thing you do is set aside time. You must feel comfortable about giving up this time. If balance is based solely on the amount of time spent and not the quality of the time — and in the beginning this often holds true — then it's worse than no balance at all. I once worked with a tremendous young tennis player. I had no doubt she would win a college scholarship and rise high in professional competition. She was not only a great athlete but she had a winning personality, warm and unassuming.

During her matches, at least one of her parents was encouraged to attend and give moral support. This became a major problem. The father didn't want to take time from work because that was his "life." But since a parent needed to be there, he showed up at the matches. He was so uncomfortable taking the time from his work that his behavior became negative. He became verbally abusive to his daughter and her opponents during matches. On one occasion, he threw a chair on the tennis court. Finally, the officials banned him from the matches. Although I didn't talk with him afterward, I'm sure he felt better at work because that's where he wanted to be. Spending time at the matches fell far short of genuine balance for the reason that he was not there in a supportive fashion. The quality of the time he spent ranked lower than zero on a scale of one to 10.

The girl's mother then was asked to fill the gap. She began attending the matches. But this took time from her social activities, which she felt were the most important things in her life. Her obsession with social doings probably exceeded her husband's obsession with work. She became rowdier than he had been. As a result, both she and her daughter then were banned from the tennis court and park. That father and mother grudgingly spent a quantity of time with no quality attached, and it significantly impacted their family in a negative way: The daughter never played tennis again. So time is not the issue. Quality is the issue.

A growing number of businesspeople and employees are attempting to deal with balance by telecommuting. They work at home two to three days a week. Some people do their job almost exclusively at home. But there is a misconception in this apparent attempt to attain balance. It is the notion that if you are in your house or in an office within the home that you have balance. Many times just the opposite happens. Though your children may be in the "office" with you, they may not be getting any quality time with you. You might assume that you have more quality time for yourself, as well: "Now I work at home. I have my computer. So I have better balance." To the contrary — when you have your workplace at home, you may spend more time working than you would if you were in a corporate environment. As a result, your balance is actually worse than it would have been if you didn't have the home office. You need to still pick your times when you are there and when you are not there.

MAINTAINING YOUR BALANCE

It is virtually impossible to get quality time if you can't find time with which to work. You need to learn to manage your time wisely — and then to balance it.

Once you have developed a good, effective time-management plan and are into the swing of the process, you will find that you are better organized, more productive and have more time to be proactive toward balance.

Note: You must accept the idea that time pressure will not end as long as you are a normal, functioning individual. You can come in early, work late, work on weekends and think about work when you are not working. But the time crunch will always be a challenge. Stressful, yes! The advantages of thriving on stress already have been discussed. Now, you learn to thrive on the stress of time management!

Here's the nitty-gritty: In order to develop balance that we can maintain, we must recognize some common barriers to time management. Here is a starter list:

Interruptions: telephones, computers; the unexpected.

Trivia.

Poor communication of decisions.

Other people's schedules.

Lack of respect for time.

Environmental factors.

Work versus home expectations.

You can start by controlling the controllable factors. This is accomplished when you follow three steps:

STEP ONE:
Keep a log for at least one week. List the things you do each day. Attach a time to each task. You will discover that your productive times will be very similar from day to day. You will also discover that conceptual, creative, productive times will be consistent across days, as will the literal, more routine tasks. This first step will help you determine when you are most productive.

STEP TWO:
Select one hour per day for a few days. Plan productive execution during that hour. Evaluate your productivity.

STEP THREE:
Share what you are doing with those people who influence your time. This is absolutely necessary. In order to achieve your desired time management and balance,

mutual respect for each other's time and balance must be developed.

FOLLOW-UP:

Continue to follow the three steps, gradually increasing the amount of time you consciously manage. Be committed to leaving free time each day to "do nothing." Once you are comfortable with what you are able to accomplish in a typical day, you might start making a "To Do" list nightly for the next day. *It is essential that you start each list with things that you can and will accomplish early the next morning* (For example: Get up. Get kids up. Pack lunches. Get kids to school. Etc.). This approach simply gets you going on your list.

STEP FOUR:

List things you want to accomplish both personally and professionally. Make two lists. "Professionally, I want to do the following. Personally, I want to do the following." Now put a time frame on your lists. Next, try to prioritize the two lists into one list. Then study your prioritized list. If it is skewed dramatically toward the job, then you have no balance or very little balance at best. If it is skewed dramatically toward your personal life, then you may have the same issue. You may have bad balance or very little balance.

HERE IS THE KEY:

For everything that's important professionally, you need something that's important personally. When you really examine why you do what you do, the personal things in your life are going to be the things that begin to take priority.

Now is the time to start achieving or restoring balance to your life. Acknowledge the need for better balance. And do something about it. Without balance, everything takes on the same importance, and when that happens there are no priorities or the priorities are inappropriate.

Take the time to make your lists of what you want to accomplish, personally and professionally. Prioritize the lists into one. Put a time frame on it — and gain the balance that will make you recognize and appreciate your total value, not only to your profession but to those in your personal life. In the final analysis, they are the most important things in your life.

GO FOR BALANCE — NOW!

THIS WORKSHEET WILL ENABLE YOU TO PRIORITIZE WHAT
YOU DO AND START DEVELOPING THE BALANCE AND TIME
MANAGEMENT THAT WILL HELP YOU WIN EVERY DAY.

<u>TASKS</u>	<u>PRIORITY</u>	<u>TIME</u> <u>REQUIRED</u>	<u>EVALUATION</u>
1.	1.		
2.	2.		
3.	3.		
4.	4.		
5.	5.		
6.	6.		
7.	7.		
8.	8.		
9.	9.		
10.	10.		

HAVE I INCLUDED:

1. TIME FOR ME?

2. TIME FOR FAMILY?

3. TIME TO EVALUATE?

4. TIME TO PLAN (TO VISUALIZE; TO ANTICIPATE)?

5. PLANS WHICH ARE CONSISTENT WITH WEEKLY GOALS?

6. HIGH-PROBABILITY-OF-SUCCESS ITEMS
AT APPROPRIATE TIMES?

7. TOUGHEST ITEMS WHEN I AM SHARPEST?

8. TIME FOR TELEPHONE CALLS?

9. TOMORROW'S PLANNING?

10. _____?

KEY 12

Search Harder —
the Wins Are in There!

WHY DO WE DO IT?

Think about why you do what you do. What are the drives, the incentives and motives behind whatever you do, both professionally and personally? What force drives you?

At this stage, in corporate America and even in the educational system, people have become very misguided and shortsighted about what constitutes winning and about why we do what we do. It has become evident that people are conditioned to define winning based solely on bottom-line numbers, or the profits or "how much money do I get out of it?" This is especially true of professionals, business people and executives. It seems that in every company if the people don't meet the goals in terms of numbers, they don't succeed. What motivates them then to continue forward?

In high-tech companies there is a trend, especially with

respect to young people who are hired, to give sizeable bonuses to attract and retain employees. If these employees don't expect future bonuses to be paid, they move to another company and get another bonus. They keep moving in order to make more money. I'm not sure what they accomplish other than material gain. I'm not sure they ever understand why they do what they do.

No wonder that some employees "fold the tent" when it becomes obvious that the numbers are falling short. Over the past 10 years, every time I have presented my program for a corporation, I have recommended that the management or ownership reward employees for small wins along the way. Everyone has long-term goals, but people need to search for short-term victories. The challenge is to give people incentives for the short term so they will stay on track and achieve the longer-term goals.

Winning does not usually jump out at you. You have to look more at the process as opposed to the bottom line. You may execute correctly, even flawlessly, and still not win on the scoreboard. So it is not difficult to understand why survival has become so popular. In the corporate world it can be quite difficult even to recognize wins, especially in the face of adversity and in light of the fact that too many people spend a significant amount of time trying to not fail.

The point of this chapter is that we have to look for wins, find something every single day that's positive. That something will drive you to the next day. *Every day you can find something that motivates you or that enables you to motivate someone else.*

HOW MOTIVATION WORKS

Motivation occupies a central place in American society. Motivational speakers tell people how good it feels to reach down and get the power within, and to visualize success. Cable TV is filled with motivational programs. You've seen them. Someone assures you that you can make millions of dollars by buying property with no money down or some other fantastic idea. Almost without exception, the aim is to get you involved with some attachment to material gain. American society is very much attached to material gain — bigger houses and cars, more cars, second homes, country club memberships. You name it; we're motivated to try to achieve it.

Motivation is used in business and industry to increase worker productivity — there is no question about it. Cars, vacation trips, money and other things are offered as incentives to high performance. I've had many opportunities to speak at awards meetings where the top salespeople were rewarded for performance. Everything is based on sales numbers. The rewards are not based on being a significant part of the team. They are not based on internal fulfillment. They are entirely based on numbers.

Parents use motivation to persuade their children to eat vegetables or to clean their rooms, and anyone with teenagers knows that's not an easy task. Businesses use motivational techniques to convince consumers to buy their products. It's a part of the marketing world. In an era when most companies offer good products, marketing separates the winners from the survivors and the winners from the losers. Competing corporations spend millions attempting to motivate customers to buy their products.

The role of motivation in the educational process is also widely recognized, although it is rarely as effective as it should be. But motivation certainly is essential to the learning process. It is the key. How many students have a good answer to these questions: "Why learn to read? Why learn math? Why learn about science? Why take social studies? Why exercise?" Most kids, even those who perform well, would join in asking, "Why study history? It's dull and boring." Students must have strong motives for doing those things. Whether it is in school or in the corporate environment, people can be placed in learning situations — but if they are not motivated, they will not learn.

Of course, motivation varies widely from one person to another even in the same situation or circumstances. What motivates one person may very well discourage another person. What motivates an athlete one day, a businessperson one day, may have no effect at all the next day. And keep in mind that when we try to motivate people, we use the things that motivate us. Don't walk away discouraged, unable to understand employee "A" not being motivated by something because it always motivated employee "B." What motivated you will not necessarily motivate another person.

MOTIVATING THE ENVIRONMENT

Many people are motivated by just being a part of a team or an organization. The problem is when they have a survival mentality and only want to be a part of the team and don't want to be a risk-taking, visible player. Because then when the team decides to move to the next level, these people are going to be left behind. Other people are not motivated at all unless they are out front, unless they control the team, unless they are very visible members of the team. Every environment, whether it's a personal environment or corporate environment, offers opportunities for both postures. You must first decide where you want to be and what you want to be. Then try to find the environment that enables you to fulfill whatever your basic needs might be.

Many businesses work hard at achieving a high comfort level for employees. People have a need to feel comfortable in the environment, so if you are going to have a winning team, you need to create a positive culture. This motivates people to stay with you because they feel good about the place they work. This also means they will feel they can make a difference, that they have a purpose in their jobs. There are many very positive environments built and sustained by people talking about the environment and thus attracting other people to that same environment.

It's true not only at work but in the home or on the athletic field. You can create an environment that people talk about. They talk about how enjoyable it is and how their part is important. That's how you start to build a positive culture.

TIMING: THE CRITICAL FACTOR IN MOTIVATION

Regardless of what technique is used, timing is probably the most critical factor in motivation. Motivation at an inappropriate time is no more valuable than the absence of motivation. It may even be more harmful to performance than no motivation at all. Mistimed efforts at motivation have an artificial air about them.

To be effective, motivation has to occur when the participant, whether in business or sports or family, will most benefit from a feeling of recognition or success. When a person has done something very good in the corporate environment, it may not be a good idea to wait until the next month to recognize the person. I think it should be done right away, almost immediately. The timing is critical. We need to do something or say something that is going to take that person to the next level and motivate him or her to continue to the next level of performance. If you don't, and the timing is off or inappropriate, then you stand a chance of losing ground. If you don't do it until a month later, you stand a chance of losing two to three weeks of productivity from people. Immediate recognition, which brings immediate motivation, is the rule of thumb as opposed to waiting and trying to pick the right time or letting time make a decision that is not effective at all.

Learn how to avoid using motivational comments when they are not appropriate. Here is how I describe this type of negative phenomenon: *When the need for the use of motivation by the person in charge outweighs the performer's need for external motivation, performance can actually suffer.* The owner of a professional sports team has a motivational type of personality. In many respects this is a positive trait, but it has a drawback. Repetition can become a negative. Sometimes the motivational comments lose their appeal when it's the same message every day about "where we are going and what we are going to do." Parents are all too-familiar with the phenomenon of children who seem to have become deaf to all advice and suggestions. You need to be very cognizant of the timing of your motivation, whether you are in the sports, the corporate or the personal world.

EXTRINSIC VS. INTRINSIC MOTIVATION

Let's look at motivation another way. You are either *extrinsically* motivated or *intrinsically* motivated. Extrinsically motivated essentially means that you are driven by material gain. Intrinsic motivation, on the other hand, means that you do things for some ideal reward. Because people generally are materially oriented, everything they do seems to have some extrinsic motivator attached to it.

Americans are in danger of forgetting their roots. Where once there were few, if any, external rewards, and Americans got an intrinsic gain from participating in different activities and from trying to achieve things, now most gain is material. When we forget where we come from, material gain takes on a life of its own. Most people very seldom spend any time thinking about the intrinsic value in what they do. So they are driven by the extrinsic motivators.

Today's children often reflect the shift from intrinsic to extrinsic motivation. Children in years past did things because they were the right things to do. They did things for parental approval and peer approval. Now children tend to do things for money. They want to be paid for the things that we used to do simply because we wanted to do those things.

The trend to emphasizing extrinsic rewards is permeating the educational system. It is no wonder that when kids get out of school and move into the workforce, their sole purpose is to gain materially. Education promotes extrinsic rewards.

You get rewards for accomplishing things. You get extra time off from school if you do certain kinds of things. You get extra points if you accomplish certain levels. Those are material gains. Those are extrinsic rewards. They are not intrinsic rewards no matter how they are positioned in school systems.

The trend affects kids in sports. If you attend a baseball game played by youngsters who are five, six or seven years old, you will see the coaches gather their teams after the game and give the game ball to the "player of the game." That's not the best idea, in my view. The preferred approach is to say that every kid played hard, tried to play well and, it is to be hoped, had a good time.

But it is amazing how kids, not to mention parents, get so excited about the "player of the game." Some parents get upset if their kid is not chosen the "player of the game." Believe it or not, I have seen parents get into fights after games over whose kid got the game ball. And then the kids get trophies at the end of the season. Some of these trophies are so big that kids can't carry them. And they get used to that emphasis on the material.

Young athletes now are recruited by different high schools. College kids get cars, money, clothes and any number of things to go to big-name colleges and play sports. After they graduate or stay four years and leave, they get huge bonuses to take jobs with certain companies. Everything seems to be materially oriented. We need to get back to learning for the sake of learning, though I realize that is an ideal view. But children need to find ways of being fulfilled by things other than extra points and the other kinds of rewards that are offered.

So don't neglect intrinsic motivation, both for your children and yourself. If you are intrinsically motivated and you achieve things that are fulfilling to you, then sufficient material things will come. If on the other hand your sole purpose is for material gain, I am not sure you learn the things you need in order to be successful in the long term. And I am not sure that you gain the team loyalty and respect that you are going to need when you encounter adversity.

Here are three things to remember about motivation:

1. Recognize that motivation is necessary for performance. Whether it is cognitive performance or physical performance, everybody needs motivation and everybody has a certain level of motivation. The question becomes whether it is a significant level, whether a person is overmotivated or undermotivated. Remember, overmotivation is less effective sometimes than no motivation at all.

2. Remember that intrinsic motivation is what you are striving for — the motivation to perform an activity or whatever it might be for its own sake — for the enjoyment. Extrinsic motivation, on the other hand, again, is obviously for material gain. We see tremendous growth in extrinsic rewards and not much growth in intrinsic motivation, and it is a disturbing trend in society and both personally and professionally for individuals.

3. You need to be familiar with as many variables as possible that might influence performance if you are going to motivate people. If it is in sales and there are 10 salespeople, those

10 people might require 10 different motivators to get to the same goal. You need to be as familiar as possible with what pushes people's buttons in order to motivate them.

If you are a parent of three or four children, you will see that they are motivated in three or four different ways. Parents need to recognize those differences and treat their children as individuals and be consistent with their motivation. For some people, whether children or businesspeople, verbal comments may be a strong motivator. For other people in the same situation, visual rewards, charts and graphs and comparisons may be motivators. For some people, just the need to compete is motivation, whether it is competing against norms or against their own records or other people. Changing your routine can also be a motivator. Other motivators are being able to focus; being able to visualize; being able to thrive on stress and knowing that you can thrive on stress; and being able to control your emotions at a high level. All those things at some point serve as motivators to become better. And remember that one of the strongest motivators we have, both personally and professionally, is positive expectation.

DIGGING FOR THOSE WINS!

So, we need to be motivated, and part of that motivation comes from finding the wins: It's what keeps us going. Part of winning is digging for those wins. You have to look for those wins. You have to analyze every situation every day. Here is my guarantee — and I seldom give guarantees: If you try, if you dig, if you look, you can find something every single day that's positive.

If you are in a corporate environment, for example, and

it's been a bad day and people haven't accomplished very much, you can dig really hard and find something good that happened. Someone made it happen. So when that person leaves the office, just remind him or her of whatever it was, no matter how small. Then that person can walk out of the door with something positive and come back the next day looking forward to accomplishing something good.

If you are in the sports environment dealing with kids — in baseball, for example — you can take the positive approach to enhance the experience for the youngsters. Sadly, too often the reverse is true. I have seen coaches discipline kids for striking out by making them do push-ups and run laps around the field.

The better approach is to talk with the kids about what they do right. The coach would get much better results if he told a youngster who struck out: "Hey, at least you swung the bat, and if you swing the bat enough times, you are going to hit the ball."

If a kid misses a ball that is hit to him, and he knocks it down, picks it up and throws it, so he missed it but made a good throw. You have to look — and look hard sometimes — to find the good, because it's so easy to get frustrated when things are not going well. If nobody else involved has that outlook, you need to be the person to pull out the good things and to show how many good things actually went on.

Here are some of the ways you can search for those wins:

1. The next time circumstances seem to be closing in on you, take a few minutes and list some things that you usually take

for granted. List some things that make you a winner — your health, home, food, friends, family, faith, the ability to express yourself, the ability to recover from adversity, past wins to think about, a promising future, the free enterprise system and the freedom to go and do what you want. Those positive things in the environment are all incentives that should enable you to move ahead. Too many times we take those things for granted.

Your list could go on and on. That's only a few of the things that come to mind. It is so easy and natural to focus on the things that we failed to do as opposed to the things we did or to focus on what we don't have as opposed to the things we have. You make a choice. You either look at everything superficially and live with that, or when necessary you dig deep and find the things that drive you to the next level.

2. Sit and chat with some older people, some who are in their 80s and 90s. You will quickly realize that when they talk about significant things in the past, most of those things brought personal fulfillment. They don't usually talk about money and material things. They talk about life. When it's hard to find wins sometimes financially, look for those personal things. Sometimes older folks can help you do that. I think the common threads that run through most of those conversations involve love, family and friends, health and exercise.

3. In searching for wins, don't bet your very existence on one event. People get so caught up sometimes when it comes to motivation and looking at wins that they attach themselves to one thing. Then if that thing doesn't work out, their whole

world begins to crumble. There have been times in the sports environment when I have been caught up in the pursuit of a world championship with a team, or winning a division with a team or even winning a game when I was working with an individual player. The problem is that you get tunnel vision and don't recognize the other good things going on around you. Beware that you don't get so caught up in an event that you only look at the end result and not the process. There's a cliché about wins: "Take them when you can get them." You have to recognize them first in order to do that. People get so hung up on what I call "The Big One." It's greatly overrated. If we accomplish the small things along the way, then the big one will take care of itself.

4. To dig for wins, you need to play to win every day in every endeavor. It doesn't matter at what level you are playing or what you are trying to accomplish. Try to do it as well as you can possibly do it. Identify common threads, for example, that may run across several days that might give you a daily lift. When adversity hits your system, call on one of these events or people to help you get back on track. (This is all a part of the speedy recovery from adversity that we talked about extensively in Key 7.)

5. It is important to diversify your interests both inside and outside the workplace so that you don't always look for wins in the same place every day. This enables you to increase the probability of winning and to balance the quality and quantity of your wins. In a whole series of superficial wins, obviously the quantity is going to be large,

but what of the quality? A couple of quality wins are better than a ton of very superficial wins.

What kind of reward are you looking for? What do you need for fulfillment? What motivates you? Use the worksheet on the following pages to identify and evaluate your motivation. It will help you to dig for the wins in your life.

MOTIVATION WORKSHEET

A. WHAT MOTIVATES ME?

1.

2.

3.

4.

5.

**B. WHAT MOTIVATES MY SUPERVISOR
(MANAGER, EMPLOYER)?**

1.

2.

3.

4.

5.

C. WHAT MOTIVATES MY SUBORDINATES?

1.

2.

3.

4.

5.

D. WHAT MOTIVATES MY CUSTOMERS?

1.

2.

3.

4.

5.

E. WHAT MOTIVATES MY SPOUSE?

1.

2.

3.

4.

5.

F. WHAT MOTIVATES MY CHILDREN?

1.

2.

3.

4.

5.

CONCLUSION

Back to the Magic!

SO HERE'S THE PROGRAM

As a quick summary, take one more look at the twelve keys to coming in first, to being a winner at whatever you do:

Key 1: Know your assets and liabilities.

Key 2: Buck the system and *expect* to win.

Key 3: Set goals — and do *better* than the best you can.

Key 4: Define your team — surround yourself with good people.

Key 5: Focus — zero in on your target.

Key 6: See it correctly with *mental* practice.

Key 7: Learn to recover — *fast.*

Key 8: Find the mental edge and win with emotion.

Key 9: Learn to thrive on stress.

Key 10: Create the right environment for winning.

Key 11: Find your balance — and keep it.

Key 12: Congratulate yourself for your wins — and let them keep you motivated.

That's the program — except for one final thing that you must never forget. *Get back to the magic!*

THE PURSUIT OF DULLNESS

There is no doubt that many people have lost the "magic." Too many people are not having fun being successful. The relentless "pursuit of dullness" seems to be the norm more often than not.

Some people seem almost embarrassed to be winning. More and more, I see people who are reluctant to show pleasure or to be happy at what they do. Think about these questions: Why did you start doing what you do? What has changed about you or others or the environment since you started?

Emotional fulfillment seems to have taken a back seat to material gain. We must get back to the emotional magic that made us who we are. If we will do this, our material gain will multiply.

A recent comment from a prospective client, who wanted me to give a convention speech, hit me in the face with the "pursuit of dullness" as I call it. He had a problem with the use of humor in my presentation.

"Your tape was entertaining," he told me. "But we don't want that to take away from the message."

"Helping people laugh is part of the message," I responded. It's all part of the magic — laughing, feeling good, enjoying what you're doing and where you are. If people walk out after my presentation with the feeling that there was something magical about what happened — something special, something that tweaked their system, maybe just some common sense they had forgotten — then they are better than they were when they walked in.

LAUGH! CRY! THINK!

But finding the magic and keeping it can only be done by working at it. People don't seem to naturally pursue the magic.

My life insurance agent, who is one of the brightest people I know, is very successful at what he does. He attends a lot of seminars. He has told me time and time again: "If I go and sit for eight hours for $100 and I bring out one idea that's going to make me better, then it's money well spent."

That's the idea of keeping the magic in what you do, keeping it exciting. The natural inclination is to fall into a routine, or a rut, and lapse into a survival mode. And in the survival mode, there's no magic at all. You only get that special feeling of magic — and it is so exhilarating — when you are playing to win and playing to win on a regular basis.

The late Jim Valvano, who coached North Carolina State to a national basketball championship, was not only a tremendous motivator as a coach, but he was a masterful speaker. When he was near death with cancer, he spoke on national television at the ESPY awards, the annual sports awards presented by the ESPN television sports network. I will never forget his comments. He said that every day we need to laugh, we need to cry and we need to think. What I took from that was that he was telling me that every day we need to stretch our emotions, every day we need to run the gamut of emotions.

That's how we keep magic in our lives. We learn to appreciate things emotionally. We need to learn to express emotions, not bottle them up all the time. Listen, it's okay to cry at sad movies. It's all right to laugh at jokes and at funny things. It's not a bad idea to go to a movie just to be entertained and not look for a message. We need to have around us things that stimulate laughing, crying and thinking on a daily basis. People may think a little every day, but very seldom will they run the gamut from laughing to crying. And they may think only when they have to. So we need to get back to those three things to find the magic.

Atlanta Braves Manager Bobby Cox creates that special feeling in the environment for his team. He respects emotion in his players. He appreciates team humor. He is very compassionate when dealing with players' personal and professional concerns. Every player feels like an essential part of the team. Players who have played for the Braves and then gone with other teams invariably say the same thing about Cox: "If you can't play for Bobby Cox, you can't play." The comment itself makes players want to be part of the Atlanta Braves team.

Think about the mystique of Notre Dame football. Notre Dame doesn't need to do a lot of recruiting of players because there is a magic, a mystique about that institution. The way the university is perceived by people is part of the magic. Players want to go there. But the perception is based on the emotional connections of a winning tradition tied to very specific events.

A company or team with magic is a place where, when you walk in the door, you feel it. There's something special in the air. Even if you're not having a good day when you walk in, you will leave feeling good. That's in the environment. It's not what people say. It's not what people do. But there's an excitement about what they do, and they all want each other to do well. Again, "excitement" involves emotions. To repeat a point: It takes everybody on a team to create this magic and sustain it. But it only takes one person on the team to destroy the magic that makes them what they are.

One factor that keeps the magic in an environment is continuity and tenure of people, people who stay with and grow with their company, and enjoy what they are doing all along the way. They see things change, and they are able to relate that to younger people coming into the business, telling them, "Where we were, where we are, and where we are going." They are good ambassadors and public relations people for the company. They have helped their companies keep a kind of magic in the atmosphere, the environment.

EMOTIONS ARE NECESSARY FOR MAGIC

In my nearly three decades of involvement with sports, I have discovered a powerful truth: *It is the magic, the emotional attraction that draws people to events.*

Unfortunately, America seems to be losing that magic not only in sports, but in the business environment and elsewhere, because loyalty has taken a back seat. And maybe it doesn't even have a back seat. Loyalty may be hanging on to the bumper about ready to fall off. Loyalty is in short supply in the corporate environment, and there's no loyalty in the sport environment. It's hard to feel good about going to a sporting event because you don't dare emotionally attach yourself to any of the athletes because they may be gone inside a year or two. They know that, and as a result you see a lot of individual performances as opposed to team play.

When I was growing up in Tennessee the only team we got on TV was the New York Yankees. So I became a New York Yankees fan. They had Mickey Mantle, Joe Pepitone, Tony Kubek, Bobby Richardson, Yogi Berra, Whitey Ford and so many other great players. I never had to look at the newspaper when spring training came around to find out who was on the team. That was a given. The same guys who were on the team the year before were on it the next year. Mickey Mantle was going to be in center field. That's the way it was. That's the way it was supposed to be. And it was that way with every team. Whatever your team, you knew who the players were and what positions they played year after year.

Then came free agency, allowing players to move from team to team. And I'm not putting players down for pursuing free agency. That's the system. But it delivered a virtual knockout to loyalty. Loyalty to the team — and to the game — has been lost on the way to the bank.

Consequently, sports have become a business proposition to an almost alarming degree. That has turned the environment into what you find in most other businesses: The game becomes a job for the players. They do their jobs and they go home. They may not feel any magic or project any magic. If they do, watch out or somebody with a "this is just another job" mindset will squelch the excitement, the emotion, the magic.

Let's go back to what happens in your own life: what caused you to start doing what you do?

What causes you to continue doing what you do? What draws you or has drawn you to your environment? What causes you to be excited about your children? Even though without question they will drive you over the edge and keep you there, at the same time they are the most exciting things in your life, they are wonderful to have and wonderful to be around. The magic is there, and it is emotionally based, isn't it?

I have two young daughters, ages four and seven, and two sons who are 12 and 15. Every day when I get up, there's magic in my life because of those children. There's a feeling, a special environment, a special atmosphere. When people come to visit, I want them to feel better when they leave than when they arrived, to feel some of the magic. Many times my children are part of that feeling.

After a visitor had spent some time with our family, I ran into him a couple of weeks later, and his comment to me confirmed that the magic is there. "There was just so much love in your house," he said.

You can imagine how much that meant. It's not something that you talk about or put on the walls in phrases and plaques and such things to motivate people. It's much deeper than that. It is about love and loyalty.

Companies that have gone through restructuring or reengineering, that have cut back on employees, in the process often become less profitable. The problem may be that they have drained the positive emotions from the environment. They have restructured not only the company, but essentially restructured the culture. I realize that it's a necessary step in many cases and must be done in order to get leaner, meaner, stronger and more focused. But there should be a concerted effort to rebuild the lost emotions in order to get more from those people who are remaining in the company. Those are the people who are going to move the company to the next level.

The same thing holds true in your family. When there is a change in the family structure, when there are more children or when somebody is gone, you have an emotional response. It is a natural consequence. When you have change, you have an emotional response. Then you have a responsibility to guide that emotional response so that it has a positive impact on the environment and on the people in the environment. That positive impact becomes the magic.

MAGIC ISN'T FAR FROM FUN

It is critical that we put the fun back in our lives. I don't mean you have to laugh and hug and scream. I mean that every day you need to find fulfillment in what you do, professionally or personally. That's putting the fun back in our lives.

When you visit Disney World, be sure to search out the Rainforest Café, one of the most magical environments I have ever visited. It simulates a forest with elephants and gorillas and other wild animals. All the time they move. They blink their eyes. They make sounds. You hear the sound of rain all the time and about every 20 minutes the lights go out and it thunders and lightning flashes, and then the rain noise gets harder all around you. When you leave, you can't wait to go back. I could go to the Magic Kingdom every year, do the same things and love it every time. I could probably go every day and love it because of the music they play. It's uplifting. And because of the enjoyment of just watching the children — and the adults — having a good time. I don't believe anyone could walk out of there and not feel good about the experience.

We need to adapt that sort of excitement and magic to our own environment. I don't mean you should have wild animals prowling around the office or have thunder and lightning piped in. But you need to determine what can be done to make the place exciting and enjoyable, a place where people want to be. To reemphasize a point: Businesses spend a lot of money motivating people but should devote more serious efforts to creating a positive environment where motivated people want to be. In short, have some fun.

Contrary to popular educational beliefs, having fun is not a deterrent to intelligence or to learning. In truth it is much easier to learn if you are having fun in the process. Nothing is more detrimental to learning than a negative environment. Having fun or enjoying yourself is the commonsense approach of intelligent people to business challenges. Indeed, winning and coming in first result, in large part, from exercising common sense.

One of the most important secrets about finding the magic is this: *Each person must feel that what he or she does is the greatest and most rewarding thing that person can imagine doing.* I feel that I have the greatest job in the world. I feel that I am blessed to have four marvelous children, a wonderful wife and exceptional in-laws. I think everybody should have that same feeling about his or her respective lives, families and professions. You should feel that what you do is the greatest job in the world and that your friends and your family and the members of your personal team are the greatest people in the world to have around you.

Let me tell you another secret: Even if you have reservations about some of these, I will promise you unequivocally that if you start thinking of them as the greatest, you will begin to experience the feeling and discover the magic that goes with it.

Corporate management will reap unbelievable benefits by creating a work environment where people have fun and where everyone feels what he or she is doing is the most important thing in the world.

WHAT TO AVOID AND WHAT TO DO

Beware of losing the magic or not finding it if you do certain things. Here are the things that I refuse to do because they will take away from whatever magic I have in my life:

1. I don't put my head underwater.

2. I don't fly if I can get there any other way.

3. I'm not dishonest with friends or others.

4. I don't cross my wife when she is on a mission.

5. I don't let strangers shine my shoes or wash my car.

6. I don't waste an opportunity to laugh or to cry or to think.

7. I don't let failure derail my optimism.

There are also certain things that I do. It is a shorter but more significant list.

1. I expect good things to happen every day.

2. I teach our children to respect themselves and others.

3. Every day, I think about my dad who died several years ago, and I miss him every day.

There is something special that happens when I think about my dad. I call it magic. I can't put my finger on it, but remembering him every day causes me to try to move forward and to do things that I think he would be proud of. Everybody needs that. I don't think you ever get too old to be responsible and feel accountable to your parents. My mom is 75 and I am 56, and she still checks on me after trips. That's a wonderful thing because Mom is still the boss. And there's magic in that, too.